BANK
HOLIDAY
ON
PARNASSUS

BANK HOLIDAY ON PARNASSUS

a litter of competitions

BY

ALLAN M. LAING

George Allen & Unwin, Ltd.

First published in 1941

PRINTED IN GREAT BRITAIN BY
STEPHEN AUSTIN AND SONS, LTD., HERTFORD

INTRODUCTION

This is an age of aces, an era of top boys. Some come to the top destroying Messerschmidts, others in building tanks or in sending merchant tonnage to the bottom; others hold the record for being bombed out, for being trapped under débris or obtaining cigarettes. Simultaneously with the Peace Conference, there will be, I always hope, a huge Old Boys' gathering of our variegated winners after the war, and if there is, I shall intrigue for the author of this book to be elected to the Chair. Mr. Laing may not have spectacular feats and sufferings to his credit, but he is distinguished among the top boys of the decade not by one astounding stunt, but by coming quietly and persistently top every week, sometimes two or three times a week. He has won more first prizes in newspaper competitions than any other man in England. Never has a man enclosed stamped and addressed envelope for reply with greater effect. The rest of us, seeing that depressing sentence : The Editor's decision is final, have groaned that we knew there was a snag somewhere. Not so Mr. Laing: those words must always have got him out of his seat and half way to the platform, in eager assurance of the editor's decision.

Alas, I imagine that up to now this distinction cannot have brought fame to Mr. Laing. Brains, not luck, turned him into a winner, and the sporting instincts of the British Public forbid it to admire the intellect. It is one thing to scoop the Pools or to be 'the first correct entry opened' in the Crosswords; quite another to beat everyone else at a parody of Kipling, a Clerihew about artists, a limerick on the Oxford Group, or at supplying the Nazis with a revised version of the ten commandments. That kind of achievement does not get one into the headlines, but—and perhaps the fame is more lasting—it does get one into the tail pieces. The genius who wrote

> How odd
> Of God
> To choose
> The Jews

has a permanent niche. No anthology could do without him. Mr. Laing's:

> When they found Giotto
> blotto
> he said: "Some twirp's
> doped my turps."

has a similar claim. Indeed, the future collector of the peculiar English art of nonsensical writing will find in Mr. Laing's pages many lines that follow the eccentric tradition of Lear, Carroll, Chesterton, and Belloc, and do honour to it. I would especially draw the reader's attention to the parodies which compare with the best of Squire's in our time. Here is Omar Khayyam on a Grand National Commentary:—

> I sometimes think that never grew the Hair
> Kept on by Commentators of the Air;
> That every Broadcast from a Field of Sport
> Takes off a Tuft the Voice can hardly spare.

His Swift, his Herrick, his Swinburne, his Sheridan and Henry James are caught with an original wit and wicked scrupulousness; while his Charles Kingsley shows that extra spurt of virtuosity which distinguishes the inspired comedian from the obedient hack. As I have said, this book is a gold mine for the anthologist of quips, shafts, retorts courteous and entertainment. To the insomniac, the browned off, the baled out, the man in the street, the man in the Anderson, the unhappy man in a Mess, the fire watcher without a fire, and the defence worker who finds so few of the intellect's civilities in the yawning hours of civil defence, Mr. Laing's fireworks and innuendos give a pleasant surcease.

On the personal side there is little but legend. Not having met their top boy ever, the Brains Trust of Great Turnstile and other learned places have exhausted many conjectures. "At a place in the North of England" Mr. Laing is said to be known, but the evidence is slight. For a time it was thought he was a syndicate; once or twice we imagined him to be a medium in profitable contact with Lear, Carroll, and G. K. Chesterton. The idea that he was a child prodigy, a sort of Hampdenshire wonder, held until he himself dropped the hint that he was a soured and persecuted nonagenarian. We came, after long deliberation, to the conclusion that he was trying to put us off the scent. In our gaudier editorial moments we have thought of starring him as The Mystery Man, The Original Mr. X, one of the Big Four (or Five or Six), the Abominable Snowman whose baffling footprints appear every week, unidentified, on the crisp slopes of the wittier side of Parnassus. But the question: Who is this Mr. Laing who regularly triumphs over every intellectual torture editors can set him, has led to such delightful speculation, that we should not care to see it end. Here is "the heap of all his winnings": if you, reader, can surpass him you, too, "will be a Laing, my son". But it seems unlikely.

V. S. PRITCHETT.

PREFATORY NOTE

This book is a one-man anthology. Its items in prose and verse were almost all elicited by the weekly literary competitions organized by the *New Statesman*, the *Spectator*, the *Listener*, the *Observer*, the *Manchester Guardian*, and the *Yorkshire Post* (to the editors of which I hereby offer the usual acknowledgments).

Many of the entries selected for reprinting have already appeared triumphantly in the prize list; but others, which merely scored moral victories, are also included.

I have not thought it necessary to state the formal terms of each competition; but if there should be any critic so amiable as to find items here and there too short, he might bear in mind that practically all the entries were under the restriction of a word- or line-limit.

One more warning. I should be sorry to have all the opinions expressed in the following pages fathered on me. Of the many parts which a successful competitor must play, that of devil's advocate is one of the commonest.

A. M. L.

CONTENTS

I
IMAGINARY CONVERSATIONS

A NEW NOTE IN ADVERTISING

JOYCE'S BOUDOIR

JOAN (*listlessly*). I don't know what's the matter with me. My conversation's completely run down. Even Jack doesn't listen to me now.

JOYCE. You funny child! It's easy to see what's wrong with *you*.

JOAN (*on the defensive*). Oh, you needn't say I'm taking the wrong dope. I take a dose of Eliot every morning, and no one could be more regular with her Powyses than I am.

JOYCE (*tenderly*). Darling: aren't you being the least bit Georgian? You might as well be taking Shaw. Now I'm going to give you a note to Mr. Gerald Gould. Promise me you'll do what he says?

MR. GOULD'S CONSULTING ROOM

GOULD. As I thought. Imperfect elimination!

JOAN. I beg your pardon?

GOULD. Your mind is failing to get rid of its Waste Lands. You can't expect to be the life and soul of a party if your brain pores are clogged with yesterday's literature. Now, my dear young lady, just go away and take a chapter of this book before every social engagement. Three guineas, please.

JOAN (*paying and taking the book*). Thank you, I will.

3

JOYCE. Listen to Joan! Isn't she wonderful?

JACK. Yes, bit of a change, what?

JOYCE. Rather! You see, she's been reading James Thurber's *Middle-aged Man on the Flying Trapeze*.

JACK. Has she, by Jove! I'll have to get a copy myself.

JOYCE. Do. It's ripping stuff, and so easy to take. Not even the most sluggish mind can resist it.

THE PROPOSAL

(From a Diary)

Was ass enough to suggest spot of matrimony to Mabel. She said: "Pardon?" I repeated the suggestion in words of one syllable, so to speak. She said:

"Marry? Who?"

I said: "Me."

She said: "You?"

I said that was the idea.

She said: "Have I got this straight? You want Me to Marry You?"

I said: "That's right."

She said: "You must be potty."

And that was that. Too Wodehouse.

SIR GREGORY PARSLOE AND THE PRAWNS

(Being a Fragment from the Hon. Galahad Threepwood's Unpublished Memoirs, rescued from the Flames)

Those who have seen how dignified my old friend, Sir Gregory Parsloe, can look on the political platform nowadays, can have no idea of how bonhomous a bean he was in the gay nineties. I know no one who sowed a fruitier wild oat. In those days Fish-Face (as we called him) had a rather low passion for prawns, preferring, if

4

I remember rightly, P. serratus to P. squilla, the former being a crustacean with more body. One evening he and I were passing, like the syncopation birds, swiftly from bar to bar, when Fish-Face suddenly announced that he was hungry and demanded prawns.

"Sorry sir," said the barman. "No prawns."

"No prawns?" said Fish-Face.

"No, sir. No prawns."

"Not even Palaemon squilla?"

"No, sir. Not even Palaemon squilla."

At this point a Rum Hot leaned over and mentioned casually that the Regent's Park aquarium had a few specimens of P. heterochirus, two feet long.

"Two feet long?" said Fish-Face. The Rum Hot nodded.

"Liar!" said Fish-Face.

"Not at all," said the Rum Hot, and whispered something in Fish-Face's ear.

"I'll do it!" said Fish-Face, and . . .

(Here, alas, the fragment ends)

HOLLYWOOD SHAKESPEAR

SCARAMOUNT CHIEF PUTS US WISE TO THE FILM OTHELLO

"This W. Shakespear of yours," Mr. Abe Putzenheimer told me, "was all there and one over; and we don't propose to de-viate a whole lot from his scenario. F'rinstance, we aim to re-tain the name part. Yes, sir. Othello is in this picture, with his sweetie, Desdemono. But he aint gonna throttle the dame, like Shakespear says, and we're cutting out the walnut juice. You can't expect honest-to-God Americans to stand for a coloured guy beating up a hundred per cent. white woman. No, sir! Now this Othello's an A1 drummer with a swell line of travel-talk. He's got a buddy, Mike Cassio, who's manager of the firm's Cyprus branch, and was Desdemono's boy friend when she was a stenog in her pop's Venice office, see? But Othello got her away from Mike with his spiels about how he put it over the Turk wholesalers. Othie and Dez get hitched and they're making fine time at the goo-goo stuff when one of the office clurks (Jago's his monniker) with the help of his crosstalk buddy, Rod, throws a spanner into the works, with some snake-stuff about seeing Dez give Mike the glad eye. Othie's on to this like a toad's tongue. Say, lissen:

OTH. What's this Mike fella to you, baby?

DES. Oh, Mike's just a friend. What's eatin' you about him, anyways?

OTH. Better lay off of him, sweetie. I ain't no patient sucker.

DES. Gee, I dunno what's on your mind. Mike's a reglar fella, and he's plumb straight. You don't think I'm sweet on him, heh?

OTH. Uh-huh!

DES. Uh-huh yourself. Can it, Othie. One husband's enough for me—at a time. Be yourself, honey, and come kiss me.

OTH. That on the level, baby? Aw, gee, you can get around a fella.

DES. Oh, and there's something else again. Just put that nosey guy Jago wise that I'm on to him, willya?

"And does he?" I asked.

"Nits," said Mr. Putzenheimer. "They stage a frameup for Jago and Rod (swell comedians both) and Rod's caught in Desdemono's hay-loft, stealing a nose rag. Othie bumps him off, but Jago's too cute and makes his getaway."

6

Mr. Putzenheimer paused and I remarked that it seemed doubtful if Shakespear would approve his alterations to the plot. Mr. Putzenheimer snorted. "A scenario writer. Hell, I should worry!"

DR. JOHNSON TALKS WITH LONG JOHN SILVER

ON THE LAUNCHING OF THE QUEEN MARY

LONG JOHN SILVER. She's a big 'un, by thunder!

DR. JOHNSON. Sir, the emphasis of an oath is not necessary to establish a matter of plain fact.

SILVER. Pipe me down, would ye, shipmate? By the powers, Old Flint himself couldn't do it, and ye may lay to that. Will she float, d'ye think?

JOHNSON. She, Sir? You take this iron nightmare for a ship? A man might as well go to sea in the dome of St. Paul's. No, Sir, she will not float.

SILVER. Easy all, shipmate. You're a landlubber, by the cut of your jib; but I know a ship when I see one. I'll take my affy-davy she's meant for the water.

JOHNSON. Sir, blind error is not mended by rash confidence.

(*The Queen Mary is launched.*)

SILVER. By thunder, she floats!

JOHNSON (*after a pause*). You are right, Sir, and I was wrong. I am but a literary cobbler and should have stuck to my last.

HITLER'S INVASION ARMADA APPROACHES

"Wots thet there smadge, Jawge?"

"Thet, Chawles, is Mr. Perishin Itlers suicide squad steamin ell fr leather fr Divy Jowneses locker. Thets wot thet is."

"Down't you be so ruddy sure, cocky. I never eard tell o naow bleedin gangsters committin suicide."

"Private Prendergawst, aw you awayah thet you aw guilty of discarridgement in the fice o the enemy? Wy, yer silly ol turnip, they downt *knaow* theyre a suicide squad, see? They think theyre a bleedin lot o conquerin eroes. But you an me, we knaows better."

"I dunno so much. Itlers wide, Itler is. Wy would e be gettin a underd thahsend of is best men scuppered fr nix? E's got sammink ap is sleeve, e as."

"Too rawt, mite. E's got the ruddy awm e serloots wiv, but e ynt got nathink else. Nah, look ere, cham. Wot eppens if thet there smadge ynt wiped aht afore it gets ere?"

"Well, wot does eppen?"

"Wy, we wipes it aht, juggins."

"An wot if they scupper us?"

"Cheer ap, cham! Theres allus the Owm Gawd, an if they fyles us in the ahr o trial, Itlerll still ev ter reckn wiv ther W.A.T.S. Therell al-ways be a Hengland."

SHAKESPEAR REPORTS A CONFERENCE

HITLER. Now sit we round this comfortable board,
My lords, and with our minds at friendly ease,
Conclude how we may hold the dogs of war
In leash perpetual. The coldest heart
Must shrink from blood's arbitrament; and we
To whose wise care full half the world to-day
Looks for salvation, dare not light war's torch.
Sir Chamberlain, what say you? Is it peace?

CHAMBERLAIN. With all my heart. Three several times
    have I,
Great Chancellor, with olive branch in mouth,

8

Flown hither like to Noah's dove, despite
Th' impatient grumblings of our English folk.
Let these my actions speak.

DALADIER.   Great Führer, I,
In France's name, applaud Lord Neville's acts
And do declare the argument of blood
Foreign to both our natures. Yet we must
Have surety for the Slovaks' lawful rights.

HITLER. You have my word. Though, like some
      irritant
Insectual, this rude and simple folk
Burrow beneath our skin, yet shall we not
Resent the sores, but full protection give
To all their reasonable hopes.

MUSSOLINI.   Well said,
My lord, and like yourself. England and France
Should now be well content. For Italy
Seals, too, this pact, which all too gentle is
To neighbours barbarous, who dare to doubt
The great intention of a greater race.

CHAMBERLAIN. Good Chancellor, the times demand
      that we
Should know with nicety what your words imply.
Do you agree that now, inviolate
And threatless of invasion and the hand
Of war, the Slovaks rest?

HITLER.   That have I said.
Let but my fair demands be met.

9

CHAMBERLAIN. And you
Will nothing add to those, nor with a harsh
And rude impatience force their laggard hand?
Remember the hard terms you now put forth
Do spell much increase on the mild demands
At Godesberg and Berchtesgaden made,
The which our strong persuasions hardly could
Thrust down the straining gullet of the Czech.
You will keep faith?

HITLER. 'Twere insult you should
doubt!
But I am tolerant, being in the right.
Set down that Germany desires but peace
With France and England, and to that great end
Doth promise honest treatment, void of force,
To all obedient Slovaks. Set that down,
I say!

CHAMBERLAIN. I shall at once, with
all dispatch.
(*Writes, then offers paper to* HITLER, *who signs.*)
Monsieur Daladier, your signature
To seal this precious peace which now we make.

DALADIER (*aside*). My heart misgives me, we'll regret
this deed! (*Signs.*)

MUSSOLINI. Nor shall the Duce lag behind, when peace
On such fair terms may be so fairly won. (*Signs.*)

CHAMBERLAIN. Now God be thanked that saves us
from a crime
And fair peace promises in this our time.
(*Waves paper triumphantly.*)
Exeunt omnes.

AN ALARMING CONVERSATION

(It is said to be the pleasant custom of certain persons to mitigate the tedium of a railway journey by arousing alarm in the breasts of their fellow-passengers by means of suitable conversations. This one is conducted in a stage whisper and stage Irish.)

"An' where did ye put the—pineapple?"

"Sure, where would I put ut but in me bag that's on the rack foreninst ye?"

"Did Shaun give ye only the wan?"

"He did so. It's he's the cautious boyo."

"Tell me, Michael, whin will ut be ripe, thin?"

"Time enough, Conal, time enough. Lave ut to me."

"It's the main secret spalpeen y'are, an' we sworn brothers. Is ut safe where ut is, d'ye think?"

"Sure, safe enough whilst me bag's sthraight up'n down; but yer sowl to Morris Kelly if the bag falls over—an' it bump'n' about for all the wurruld like Father Ryan on Phelim Donohue's ass."

"Mebbe, Michael, ye'd betther have it down. 'Twould be safer, I'm thinkin', atwixt yer knees."

"Ach, Conal alanna, it's all right, I tell ye. Would ye have wan o' these holy Luthers from the preachin' north givin' ut maybe a kick?"

"I would not, Michael. But me bowls go as wathery as Brian Rafferty's potheen ivery time the thrain rattles. Have ut down, Michael dear, or mebbe ut'll . . ."

'Wheesht, ye daft omadhaun. Ye've got nerves like Pat Hanlon's ould chandelier wid the glass bobbins itself. There, now: I'll lift ut down, an' may Michael an' all his angels kape yer big feet fr'm hoistin' us all to glory."

"Michael dear, is ut wan o' the colleges we're afther visitin'?"

"Arrah, hould yer whisht, ye switherin' gossoon, ye! Why shouldn't ut be the thrain utself, then?"

"Howly saints, Michael, don't say ut! It's jokin' y'are, surely. Is ut you an' me to be sufferin' martyrs f'r the cause? Ochone! To hear me life tickin' away like an' ould alarm clock. Ochone!"

BACON TALKS WITH SHAKESPEARE

SHAKESPEARE. Give you good day, Sir Francis.

BACON. And you, Master Brakespeare.

SHAKESPEARE. Shakespeare, an' it please you, sir.

BACON. Ay? Well, well, so be it. What's in a name?

SHAKESPEARE. Nought, Sir Francis, if it be mine, but there is much saving grace in the name of Bacon.

BACON. Marry, sir, do you play upon words? Are you one of those pestilential fellows, punsters, who let their thoughts follow upon their words, when words, as even fools know, should be servants unto thought?

SHAKESPEARE. Your pardon, Sir Francis. We writers grow great only if we tickle the ears of the groundlings, and your play upon words is ever sure to stir their ribs.

BACON. "We writers," quotha! And how earn *you* such a title, Master Br-Shakespeare?

SHAKESPEARE. A few lean verses, Sir Francis; some idle plays. Nought, since they have missed your ear.

BACON. So? Take comfort, Master Brakespeare. Grow great without me: I am no groundling. Give you good day.

WHISTLER SCORES OFF SHAW

It is odd that no one has ever told the story of Whistler's first meeting with Mr. Bernard Shaw, especially as it gave Whistler the opportunity for one of those biting comments for which he was eternally on the look-out. Anyhow, this is what happened. A friend more or less jocularly introduced Mr. Shaw with the remark: "A fellow artist, James."

"Indeed?" said Whistler, with ominous courtesy. "And what particular branch of art do you practise, Mr. Shaw?"

"Practically all of them," replied Shaw promptly, entering into the spirit of the thing. "But I am specially good at blowing my own trumpet."

"Ah, yes," Whistler nodded. "One of the bragg-arts, I think?"

DR. BUCHAN IS REPROACHED BY FLORA THE GODDESS OF SPRING

FLORA. Well, Doc., you dan me dahn proper, you an yore cold periods! Near M'y it is, an ere I yem wiv chilblynes, a cold in the ead an me eavy woollen combinytions orn!

BUCHAN. Hoots, lassie, dinna haver. Ah tellt ye the air mecht hae a wee bit nip intillt, but ye maunna pit the blame on me. Ah'm a meteorologist, no the Deity himsel.

FLORA. Gawt a nelibi, ave yer? Yah! Tryin ter be a crorss atween Old Moore's elmanec an me old pal Jupiter! S'y, wen's it gowin ter be wawm agyne?

BUCHAN (crossly). Ah canna tell ye. Mebbe a two-three days, mebbe a week. Ah'm nane o yer cheapjack astrologers. Forbye, dinna cast yer wee bit clooties till ye ken. (Stalks off.)

JACK POINT AND SERGEANT MERYLL DISCUSS THE FILMING OF THE YEOMEN OF THE GUARD

SERGEANT MERYLL. So, Jack, we are to have a new lease of life!

JACK POINT. By your favour, Sergeant, no: what they offer us is but a temporary tenancy of a *flat* in the *shades*.

SERGEANT MERYLL. Come, come, you're a melancholy dog. Doesn't this assure our future?

JACK POINT. I fear me not, Sergeant. 'Tis but a series of reflections on our past.

MR. PICKWICK'S BLACK-OUT

"It's very dark," said Mr. Pickwick, in apprehensive tones as he stepped into the coach at Blackfriars.

"Cimmerian—quite!" agreed Mr. Jingle, as they set off. " Burglar's paradise—policeman's nightmare—nightwalker's holiday—misery for hot chestnut man—lamplighters, too—out of job—*felo de se*—sad, very! All the same—compensations—artists pleased—Albert Memorial invisible—no skysigns—astronomers, O be joyful—also Love's young dream," added Mr. Jingle, with a leer, which was quite lost on Mr. Pickwick, since he hadn't yet learned to see in the dark. At this moment the coach mounted the pavement and almost upset, causing Mr. Pickwick to gasp in alarm, and forcing even Alfred Jingle to suspend his flow of conversation for a few seconds.

"No cause for alarm—careless driver—probably half-seas over," he said at last, when they had jolted safely on to the road again. "Remember—years ago—dark

night—hansom—Strand—driver tiddly—threw me out
—fell on my head—hospital six weeks—cheerful, very!"

With an air of finality, the coach stopped, and the
driver got off his box to say in surly tones that "'E ver
lorst and vot vos the parties proposin' to do about it?"

THE PHILISTINE

"Books," he said, flatly, "are a luxury in war-time."

"A luxury?" I exclaimed, rhetorical with indignation:
"Books are the food of the mind, the garment of the
spirit, the wings of hope. They are the armour of sorrow
and the ammunition of delight; knowledge flowers in
their garden; they are the air-raid shelters of memory.
And you would tax these?"

He said he would.

II
EPITAPHS, EPIGRAMS, AND INSCRIPTIONS

EPIGRAMS

DEAD POET PROVIDES MEAL-TICKET

Stratford, being Shakespear's town,
Cashes in on his renown:
Our great bard, though lapt in lead,
Still ensures his people's bread.

A REYNAUD BLOOMER

(M. Reynaud, in a broadcast, said: "In England . . they have constructed thousands of houses which are like fields of fresh flowers in the country surrounding the towns.")

It seems ungracious to a flattering friend
    The Frenchman's horticulture to expose;
But brick-box streets that stretch without an end
    To us resemble no known flower that blows:
We dare not cheer the statesmen who defend
    A wilderness that blossoms like these rows.

DISAPPEARANCE OF THE LEMON

He is a pessimist who dares conclude
    We've heard the lemon's valedictory;
For, when the war is won, we shall include
    A lemon in the fruits of victory.

A DICK TURPIN WAISTLINE FASHION

The ghost of bold Dick Turpin rides once more,
    By both his ancient passions paced;
And, failing booty in a coach-and-four
    Still lays a hand on beauty's waist.

A WINTER WINDOW-BOX

The Flow'rs that from their narrow Box peep'd out
Have gone with Autumn's Splendour, up the Spout:
   Ah, gently dig the Soil! For who can tell,
Save Time and Middleton, what yet may sprout?

THE NEW LIDDELL-AND-SCOTT

Reviséd Lexicon, wise-tongued, benign,
   You come most aptly to restore man's wit,
And prove, while warring nations seek a sign,
   The Greeks, as usual, had a word for it.

A WASTE PAPER BASKET

This basket, open-mouthed, awaits in vain
   The crumbs of literature it should have tasted,
or X., the writer, cannot face the pain
   Of knowing that a word of his is wasted.

OXFORD COCKNEYS

Cockneys' flat vowels, heard beneath Bow Bells,
   First kindled St. John Ervine's hissing fires:
The flames swept on till soon they rivalled Hell's:
   Now red tongues lick at Oxford's dreaming spires.

A MIDGE

Impartial men agree, with gnats in view,
   That Aryan purity's a rash conclusion,
For what's to stop a midge that bites a Jew
   From slyly carrying out a blood transfusion?

A HEAT WAVE

Why take on so because it's hot?
  Such conduct always makes me scoff:
My plan's to find a private spot
  And do a little taking off.

THE GUY FAWKES BLACK-OUT

When Flaming Death, in aeroplanes,
  Lets off his fireworks in the sky
What audience for Brock's or Pain's?
  Who cares a pinwheel for the guy?

EROS BOARDED UP

Blame your creator, Eros, for this fuss:
  His pose has placed you in this galley:
He should have known the human boy in us
  Could not resist so patent an Aunt Sally.

EPSTEIN, CHRIST, AND JAMES DOUGLAS

Epstein, in gratitude for life and limb,
Carved Christ in stone as God's son seemed to him.
In fitting recompense for doubtful art
God nudged James Douglas to take Epstein's part.

EPITAPHS

ON A CIVIL SERVANT

This Civil Servant made the grade
By dying in a Blitzkrieg raid:
He'd no tin hat and fired no gun,
But perished knowing duty done.

He paused upon the shelter stair
To read the notice posted there
(For how could he take cover till
He knew the departmental will?)

A simple 'temporary,' he
Misunderstood 'celerity,'
And ere he got the hang of it
A Heinkel registered a hit.

THE FIRST WASP

Here on this plate, his sting withdrawn,
  His corpse with marmalade all mingled,
Lies one who, prematurely born,
  By Fate for early death was singled.
No conquests crowned his brief career—
  Rash innocent, by spring besotted!—
His life and death are summed up here:
  He came: he saw; and he was swatted.

A RASH STATESMAN

Here lies a rash statesman whose laurels
Were earned in appeasing world quarrels:
  His tomb is erected
  By foes who respected,
But couldn't live up to, his morals.

SAGITTARIUS (OF THE "NEW STATESMAN")
(*For her tombstone*)

This poet-archer loosed her last, sharp shaft:
  A tombstone epitaph to sting her Maker:
You will not find it here, for though God laughed,
  The lines were censored by the undertaker.

NINETEEN-THIRTY-NINE

This year of suffering and strife
   Were better lapt and sealed in lead;
But while the metal still takes life,
   We may not spare it for the dead.

A PREACHER

Give thanks to Death who, to deceased's abilities,
Added the gift of terminal facilities.

A TELEPHONE OPERATOR

For God's sake her subscribers are emphatic
In hoping Heaven's Exchange is automatic.

A DOCTOR

Pilgrim to Harley-street, he bore no banner,
But jilted science for a bedside manner.

A NURSE

Restless she sleeps, in Death's great ward forlorn,
Fearing, as patient, she'll be waked at dawn.

A PLUMBER

Called to a hurry-job at High Heaven's Gate,
He left (as usual) without tools or mate.

AN AIR-RAID WARDEN

Death swooped on him and proved a private hunch:
The warden's gas-mask case was full of lunch.

A BEST-SELLER

God and his publisher are now in session
Settling the details of Brown's new impression.

AN OFFICIAL

When death was hinted, Mr. Smith grew warm
And asked for notice on the proper form.

A SOLICITOR

This man of law steered justice into port
By firmly keeping clients out of court.

ON AN UNSUCCESSFUL COMPETITOR IN THE "NEW STATESMAN" COMPETITIONS

(*To be inscribed on a plaque let into the wall of No. 10, Great Turnstile.*)

This cenotaph infers his tomb
    Who spent, within, his mental wages,
And met an almost weekly doom
    In the *New Statesman's* back-end pages.

For fifty years, week in, week out,
    He strove for competition guineas,
Only to swell the patient rout
    Of crude and uncommended ninnies.

For half a century he bore
    The crazy whims of cross-eyed judges
And, silent, suffered all the more
    From prejudice that never budges.

To the Great Turnstile in the sky
    His entries now are re-directed;
And since *Heaven's* just, his weekly try
    One day by God must be selected.

THE RUINS OF THE CRYSTAL PALACE

See, framed in steel, its crystal lights ablaze,
    The jewelled palace of a glad child's dream:
Now day dissolves it, and our yearning gaze
    Quarters a desert for the vanished gleam.

A DEAD FLY

To meet Death
with the strawberry jam on his breath;
with the lingering flavour of dung
on his tongue!
To be
crushed in the crumbs of afternoon tea
by a fluke
and a paper-backed book!
To die
and lie
where he flew as a fly,
swatted,
rotted;
and to raise a cheap laugh
even with his epitaph! . . . .
Who'll weep in the dusk a
dead musca?

ON A SOCIAL FAILURE

Beneath these jam-jarred flowers there lies
A harmless soul who longed to rise
To circles where the rich and great
Drink turtle soup from silver plate.
Alas! his sordid social sphere
Did not include a single peer;

No baronet had felt a whim
To pass the time of day with him.
He died no lordly death, of gout:
A modest Morris Minor laid him out.
(The miscreant who broke his bones
Turned out to be a Mister Jones.)

INSCRIPTIONS

FOR A TELEPHONE BOX

Within this little place of talk
   A myriad ears are in your reach:
Here separation cannot balk
   The sweet necessity of speech.

A CONCENTRATION CAMP FOR BORES

Stranger, be warned! Within these prison pales
   They pine whose ways the world could not afford:
Here Tedium with a thousand voices wails,
   And bores, with only bores to bore, are bored.

ON A PORTRAIT BY KAPP

This isn't quite the sort of chap
To be immortalized by Kapp:
He is, if I remember right,
A third-rate pug, who sold his fight;
And then, to earn his daily grub,
Became a bouncer at a pub.
There, though he hacked a pretty shin,
He mixed the job with too much gin.
When he was fired, what could be do
But join the nearest B.F.U.?

Now, armed with heavy, hobnailed shoes,
He Christianizes East End Jews . . . .
I'm glad to note his hair is thinner:
No hair should grow on such a sinner.

FOR A CASUAL WARD

You must not spit upon the floor,
Nor scribble on the walls or door;
By order, you're requested not
To lie down clothed upon your cot;
Complaints about the food you get
May not be made, will not be met;
The task that's given you to do
Is not a bit too hard for you;
You must not shirk it without cause
(See penalty in town's bye-laws);
You must not smoke, you may not drink,
You must not, beyond limits, think;
Keep every natural impulse hidden,
For one and all they are forbidden;
And if you have a mind to die,
Please do so when the doctor's by.

FOR A WILD FLOWER SANCTUARY

To shelter from the vandal's casual clutch
And to escape the grafting gardener's touch,
Destroying, or improving overmuch,
        These wild flowers came from far.
Instinctive all with nature's pure intent,
They offer glory to the eye, and scent
So fragrant, the creator must have meant
        To leave them as they are.

III
VARIETY

AN ALLURING LAST PARAGRAPH

(This last paragraph of a thriller is designed at once to stimulate and foil the lazy curiosity of those who read the end of a book first.)

"But what happened to Biddlecombe?" asked Henry, with some impatience.

"That," remarked Mr. Inkpin, in his usual precise tones, "is implicit on page one-forty-three and almost explicit on page two-two-four." And then, as Henry seemed to expect him to go on, he added:

"My dear boy, I have taken the considerable trouble of recording, in some two-fifty-six pages of quite remarkably lucid prose, the whole fascinating story of Armadaile and the Applebys. I have given you thrills and — er — um — rough stuff. I have mingled the happiness of achievement with the pleasant agony of suspense. I have not, I think, overlooked either humour or the quiet beauty of appropriate descriptive passages. Character is the backbone of my tale. But if, in addition to all this, you expect me to offer you an appendix in the form of a neat police report summary that will save you all the effort of thought, then I am afraid, my dear boy, you are going to be disappointed. No casual thumber of these pages will learn all he needs to know from a lightning glance at my final paragraph. No."

Mr. Inkpin paused, sat back in his chair, and cocked an eye at Henry. "Of course," he went on, blandly, "if you were to ask me, as your solicitor, to elucidate any point not crystal clear to your—er—um—intelligence,

I would be prepared to comply. On the usual terms. Yes."

For a moment Henry seemed about to indulge in six-and-eightpence worth, but in the end he held his tongue. Instead, he took the book the solicitor held out to him and, ignoring Mr. Inkpin's suave "Good afternoon," turned to page one and began to read it carefully once more.

FILLETED SWEARING BY FOUR FAMOUS PEOPLE

COMM. MARCONI. "You oscillating pentode!"
JULIAN HUXLEY. "You katabolic blastoderm!"
JOHN MASEFIELD. "You anapaestic assonance!"
SIR T. BEECHAM. "You augmented diatonic interval!"

A CONCERT PROGRAMME

BLITZKRIEG: or, The Land of Promise. von Deutschland's Unfinished Symphony

First Movement (*andante furioso*).

A roll of drums announces the theme, which is briskly carried on by the brass, rising presently to a crescendo of thunderous cacophony, in which the violins are scarcely heard. Fragments of national anthems are tossed about, merging into the German anthem, loud, dominant, triumphant. The land of promise is at hand!

Second Movement (*scherzo*).

The triumphal note of the First Movement is continued bravely, but has to contend soon with a derisive interpenetration from the bassoon. A serpent has entered the Eden! Soon the drums are silenced altogether, and a querulous piping of flutes strives to rise above the bearish growlings of the openly sneering bassoon. The final passages are proudly protestant as though defying despair.

Third Movement (*allegro*).

Now the violins begin to plead softly at first, with only distant threat of drums. All is not well in the Promised Land. The pleading is exchanged now for blustering brass and then for an exquisitely slow and mournful melody which gradually takes possession of the whole orchestra and terminates in an unexpected angry roll of drums over which a thin note of hope is heard from a single horn.

(*No one knows how the Fourth (unwritten) Movement was intended to be treated.*)

THE MARCH HARE: A FABLE

"You are making a mad world," said the old Lion, "where all is fighting and there is little food. I abdicate." So the animals met to choose another king; and the Wolf boasted his ferocity, the Bear his strength, the Fox his cunning, and the Owl his wisdom. Finally the March Hare piped: "These qualities, gentlemen, are irrelevant. In a mad world the maddest must be King. I am your best choice." Struck by this reasoning, the animals gave the crown to the March Hare, thus proving that

THE LOGIC OF FOOLS IS YET MORE FOLLY.

SLOGANS FOR MODERN PROPHETS

JEANS. That's eternity, that was!

FREUD. Can Hear Your Dreams Talking!

BROWNING. Gives you that Thinking Feeling.

MARX. Puts the Pro in Proletariat.

DR. JOHNSON. Is bully for blockheads.

KIPLING. The Big Noise for Old Boys.

MRS. BEETON. Beats the Best Eggs.

WILDE. For Pre-War Wisecracks.

HEMINGWAY. Touches you on the Raw.

SHAW. For Shocks and Showdowns.

HOW THE SEA SERPENT GOT ITS REPUTATION

Once upon a time there was an Ambitious Worm which, escaping the Angler's bait-can, fell into the Sea. By some freak of Creative Evolution, it survived and swelled to thrice its size. It was then flung with a load of herring on to a trawler's deck. To the Fishermen it seemed the fattest Worm they had ever seen. They killed it and threw it overboard, but it kept growing in their minds from one foot to three, from three to twelve, and from twelve to thirty; and by the time they told the Tale at home it was a Genuine Sea Serpent a hundred feet long, with twenty-five coils and an affidavit from nine eye-witnesses. Far away the Worm turned happily in its watery grave.

OVERHEARD

AT A CONCERT OF CHAMBER MUSIC

"Don't violin strings sometimes break?"

"Wrap 'em up in a picture paper, Mister. I ain't no scholar."

"Why don't they put all the really *good* books together?"

"Why, his hair's quite short!"—"Sh-sh! This is modern poetry."

THEIR FIRST RECORDED WORDS

SIR GALAHAD. A gentleman's a gentleman for a' that.

MAE WEST. A girl with my figure can't be expected to go straight.

CANON SPOONER. I hope to live up to the speed of the Crooners.

OSCAR WILDE. Nurse: has it ever occurred to you that this milk-bottle and these napkins constitute a vicious circle?

DINNER PARTNERS AND WHAT THEY TALKED ABOUT

BOADICEA and JOHN LOUDON MCADAM (Roman roads).

ELIZABETH FRY and JOHN BUNYAN (Low company).

NELL GWYNN and SHAKESPEAR (First nights).

GRACE DARLING and CAPTAIN BLIGH (Open boats).

JOAN OF ARC and the CHEVALIER D'EON (The custom of the sexes changing hats on Hampstead Heath).

ANNE HATHAWAY and SAMUEL PEPYS (Second-best bedsteads).

35

CANDIDATES FOR A NEW ENGLISH DICTIONARY

1. GARGULOUS. Example: " . . . splutterings voluble with the gargulous indignation of escaping bathwater."
2. PUNDERWITS. Example: "Thank heaven the tedious punderwits of the pre-Victorian era no longer dominate the dinner-table."
3. BLANDULATIONS. Example: " . . . the blandulations of B.B.C. announcers."
4. DUPPLE. Example: " . . . as dupple as a diplomat."

LIBRARIES

FOR A SHIP SETTING OUT IN SEARCH OF BURIED TREASURE

TREASURE ISLAND. (A spot of romance is indicated.)

THE PRAYER BOOK. (Since the burial service will be in constant use.)

A BOOK OF COMMUNITY SONGS. (To keep low spirits up.)

THE LAW OF TREASURE TROVE. (To keep high spirits down.)

THE JOURNAL OF A DISAPPOINTED MAN. (It sounds as though it might be appropriate.)

WILLIAMS ON BANKRUPTCY. (The usual treasure-hunt substitute for a happy ending.)

IMPROBABLE BOOKS BY UNLIKELY AUTHORS

SEVENTY TIMES SEASICK. By Captain David Bone.

ROUND THE WORLD ON A SCOOTER. By Teddy Brown.

THE WEALTH OF NATIONS, rendered into heroic couplets. By W. W. Jacobs.

36

FLY FISHING IN THE ANDES. By Ethel M. Dell.

WAS JEREMIAH AN IRISHMAN? By Sir Bernard Spilsbury.

ALTERNATIVE BOOK TITLES

ULYSSES: or, A Day in Dirty Dublin.

FLUSH: or, The Faithful Ba-Lamb.

BRAVE NEW WORLD: or, The Doper's Dream of Home.

LADY CHATTERLEY'S LOVER: or, Sex and Sensuality.

THE GOOD COMPANIONS: or, Isn't Life Champion?

THE GLASTONBURY ROMANCE: or, The First Cause Runs Amok.

IMPENDING AUTOBIOGRAPHIES

SHIRLEY TEMPLE. " Twinkle, Twinkle, Little Star."

HIMMLER. "Their Struggles."

JAMES JOYCE. "Me Loive an Litters."

TOSCANINI. "My Life and Times."

AL CAPONE. "No Cross, No Crown."

MACAULAY'S "HORATIUS" IN HEADLINES

"CUSS-WORD" PORSENA'S CAMPAIGN CHECKED

HOUSE OF TARQUIN FOILED

ROME SAFE

EPIC OF THE BRIDGE

THREE AGAINST THREE TIMES THIRTY THOUSAND

BRIDGE CAPTAIN HERO OF GREAT FIGHT

WITH TWO COMPANIONS KEEPS ARMY AT BAY

"NOBLEST ROMAN OF THEM ALL"

SINGS "OLD MAN RIVER" THEN, WOUNDED, SWIMS TIBER
IN FULL KIT

PORSENA PRAISES EPIC FEAT

CITY FATHERS' GRATITUDE

LORD ASTUR AMONG THE DEAD

FASCIST WOMEN TREAT GEN. SEXTUS AS CUSPIDOR

FULL STORY FROM OUR OWN SPECIAL CORRESPONDENT
AT THE FRONT
(*Pictures on Back Page*)

IV
LIMERICKS AND CLERIHEWS

LIMERICKS

AN ALPHABETIC ATTEMPT

As amblers aren't all acrobatic,
And autos are all autocratic,
    An accident Act
    ("Automobiles attacked")
Appears almost axiomatic.

IF YOU PLAIUS

A fatalist student of Caius
Having made up his mind he would freeze,
    Sat about in the nude
    And took ice with his food;
But all that occurred was a sneeze.

THE ECONOMICS OF EARTHQUAKES

Of the horrors that harrow us all
When an earthquake occurs in Nepal,
    I'm inclined to place first
    Not mere hunger and thirst,
But the price to which elephants fall.

WHO'S AFREUD?

When an obstinate fellow of Fife
Persisted in loving his wife,
    Denying obsessions,
    Bad dreams and repressions,
The Freudians feared for his life.

THOUGHTLESS

There was a young chap with a kink
Who boasted: "I don't need to think:
    God-guided I am
    Through the blood of the Lamb,
Not to mention the Oxford Group, Inc."

THE AMOEBA

The amoeba was all of a twitter
In case she should turn out a quitter:
    Would she hark back (a sob!)
    To the protoplasm blob?
Or prove, by survival, the fitter?

DROP IN SHARES?

Said a sceptical person of Lynn:
"I don't get this sharing of sin:
    'Twould be awfully nice
    To annihilate vice,
But this is just spreading it thin!"

DAMAGED GOODS

In Hollywood, home of the star,
Dumb beauties are built up to par;
    But if found second grade,
    Or in any way frayed,
How welcome at Elstree they are!

CAMOUFLAGE

There was an old person of Stiffkey
Who got himself up like a biffkey;
    But in spite of his gall
    It was plain to us all
He was just a poor priest playing hiffkey.

CLERIHEWS

When Mr. Jack Squire
was dubbed a Knight of the Shire,
he said: "It's a shame:
I feel just the same."

Mr. James Bridie
is anything but tidy:
in one play he wrote
he left a clergyman lying about.

Sir James Barrie,
after a week-end in Paree,
remarked that the reeking of its lums
failed to remind him of Thrums.

Mr. Bernard Shaw and I
were both born in July:
not much of a link,
but jolly, *I* think.

Velasquez
must not be confused with Asquith:
one was an alien:
the other produced "Pygmalion".

Sir Alfred Gilbert
said: "I'm feeling ill, Bert;
but Bert's history
is a mystery.

43

When they found Giotto
blotto,
he said: "Some twirp's
doped my turps."

Jack the Ripper
even as a nipper
had designs on the vital parts
of tarts.

Judas Iscariot
had charge of the commissariat;
but after dark
he was a copper's nark.

Guy Fawkes
used to have long talks
with Bloomsbury fellers
about best-sellers.

Samuel Pepys
said it gave him the creeps
to see Nell Gwynn beckoned
by Charles the Second.

Herr Hitler
refused to meet Emile Littler
and so never became
a pantomime dame.

Mr. Molotoff
said Turkey was off,
but he hoped to have a little isthmus
for Christmas.

Viscount Gort
has been known to snort
when he got plum-and-apple jam
with his ham.

Mr. Churchill
cannot read Virgil:
biographers with a little Latin
will always put that in.

The Coles
insisted on separate souls,
and two crosses will mark the spot
of their last plot.

The mind of Miss Dorothy Sayers
is in two layers:
criminological
and theological.

If anyone could condemn wearing combs.
at Proms,
Mrs. Henry Wood
could.

Charles Dickens
might have kept chickens,
but somehow writing
seemed more exciting.

Instead of blushing cherry hue
at having invented the clerihew,
Mr. E. C. Bentley
just smiles gently.

CLERIHEWS WITH A DIFFERENCE

Johann Sebastian Bach
cleared his brain with spinach:
to this habit is due
many a fugue.

Archimedes
didn't invent velocipedes
because (like Laocoon)
he was born too soon.

Dance hostess Terpsichore
always swore
when she got less than a stater
or had to drink water.

When Sarasate
had a date,
he usually punched a hole in
his violin.

Jenny Lind
was notoriously kind,
but she always said: "Nope!"
to accompaniments on the calliope.

The late W. T. Stead
loathed mead
and almost never drank claret
in a cabaret.

Sophocles
had a passion for cockles,
which caused scenes
between him and Diogenes.

A Mrs. Jones
was picking anemones
when the bite of a flea
gave her another idea.

V
WAR-TIME VERSES

BLACKOUT BLUES

I

A GORGEOUS ADVENTURE

(*After W. S. Gilbert*)

The house blinds are all down, and no lights in the town,
   and the moon won't be up for a week or two,
And you're out in the street, not too sure of your feet,
   and longing in vain for a peek or two,
Then you out with your flash, and it breaks with a
   crash on the stones of a hard granite gutter,
And there you are left, of all comfort bereft,
   in a darkness too utterly utter;
As you stumble along, feeling sure you are wrong,
   with no clue to assist in detection,
An unseen pillar-box gives you shrewdest of knocks,
   quite deranging your sense of direction;
Then the roadway you cross, all but taking a toss
   from a motor too silent and dim-lit,
And a curse from the car gives your pride such a jar
   that it goes through your head like a gimlet.
You're now hopelessly lost, as you know to your cost
   when you march with a bang into railings,
But the stars you set free just ensure that you see
   all your plain topographical failings;
Dropping anchor right there, you are ready to swear,
   in a mood of intense irritation,

When a chance passer-by shines a light in your eye
   and gives you your present location;
Then remarks with a smile that is guiltless of guile,
   as you're puzzling your subsequent track out:
"Between you and me—and I hope you agree—
   it's a gorgeous adventure, this blackout."

II

THE DOG WITH THE LUMINOUS NECK

Hound incorporeal,
   Haloed with light,
Aurora boreal,
   Circling the night,

How much voluminous
   Body's at rest
Back of thy luminous
   Collar, unguessed?

Wagg'st thou, unseen of me,
   Tail in the dark?
Wiser 't had been of thee
   Soundly to bark.

I, now saluting thy
   Collar bright-lined,
Might have been booting thy
   Dimmer behind.

III

A BLACKOUT REFLECTION

I love lots of light
In the windows of shops.
It's a civilized sight:
I love lots of light.
As I bus home at night
To my meal of chump chops,
I love lots of light
In the windows of shops.

IV

A LAMENT FOR LAMP-POSTS

Pithed beacon of the public ways
  That burneth now no lights,
Thou hast, indeed, known better days,
  And beamed on brighter nights.

Thou deal'st us, when we go about,
  Shrewd buffets in the dark,
And urgent dogs must smell thee out,
  Unguided by thy spark.

Yet when these sobering times shall pass
  And peace fill full her cup,
We'll share again thy lifted glass
  And be, with thee, lit up.

V

(*After Blake*)

And did these feet, in pre-war days,
   Walk along England's lighted streets?
And were shop-windows all ablaze,
   And coppers silent on their beats?
And did that Corporation bus
   Shine forth in splendour from afar?
And was it mere child's play for us
   To dodge the swiftly-moving car?

Bring me my torch of waning power!
   Bring me my phosphor button bright!
Bring me my stick—O, dreadful hour!
   That brings the darkness of the night!
I will not cease from pavement taps,
   Nor shall my stick sleep in my hand
Till I have tested all the gaps
   In England's blind and shuttered land!

BARRAGE BALLOONS
(*A Nursery Ode*)

I say, you toy balloons up there,
   That seem so proud and ride so high;
Take off that silly, solemn air:
   You're only playthings in the sky.

The world, it seems, is young again,
   And London full of grown-up boys
Who, tired of tasks that call for men,
   Have turned to nurseries for toys.

And you balloons, that masquerade
    As soldier-guards on sentry-go,
Forget how children's games are played
    Or you'd put up a better show.

Grow grins upon your solemn rumps:
    Uncoil a gaily-streaming tail:
Don't hang about like lifeless lumps
    When penny kites can soar and sail!

You have been warned: our little men
    Soon tire of toys that take no pains;
And you'll be rather sorry when
    They turn you down for aeroplanes.

THE CHARGE OF THE (MECHANIZED) LIGHT BRIGADE

There was hardly a cheer as we slipped in the gear
    And rattled at speed towards the talus,
For the Light Brigade Tanks weren't offering thanks
    For the hell that would presently hail us.

We were fifty machines—and you know what that means
    Against Jerries in concrete emplacements:
Just a handful of peas in a go-as-you-please
    With Death spouting red from steel casements.

But we called on no god as we churned up the sod,
    With the shells popping sweetly around us,
For in this sort of fair, it's Old Nick in the chair,
    And we knew that his devils had found us.

From the first it was plain that our charge was insane,
   But the Light Brigade chaps aren't quitters;
So we thundered along, with our guns going strong,
   Breathing hopes that the Jerries had jitters.

*　　　*　　　*　　　*

Well, you know how it went: we just made a small dent
   In the talus H.Q. wanted taken:
Out of fifty tanks, two, and they twisted askew,
   Returned to the lines badly shaken.

Dick Williams and me, we both got the V.C.,
   But there wasn't a ghost of a rumour
That they had on the mat the blue pencil Brass Hat
   Who committed the perishing bloomer.

BELISHA BEACONS MELTED DOWN

Beat out no dirge on muffled drums
   To speed these yellow knobs:
Let people turn down honest thumbs
   And stifle silly sobs.

"Farewell" is much too kind a word
   For such unsightly plants:
They've long been asking for the bird,
   So kick them in the pants.

Make no pretence of feeling blue,
   Of mourning, as for loss:
Let Hore Belisha wear the rue
   And take this second toss.

WHEN THE HORSE RETURNS

When motor cars forsake the street
   Unhonoured and unsung,
The first thing that the eye will meet
   Is quantities of dung.

Of all the changes in our life
   By petrol rationing rung,
This one will cut most like a knife:
   The pungent smell of dung.

The horse will clatter forth once more
   Our pleasant paths among,
While gardeners alone encore
   The consequential dung.

War's horrors all have been foreseen:
   They are on every tongue;
But who'd have thought that they would mean
   Not danger, death—but dung?

SURVIVAL OF THE FITTEST

When pennyworths have dwindled down
   To trifles microscopic,
And busmen scorn the humble "brown"
   With language almost tropic,

When every penny slot-machine
   Puts up its simple prices,
And Stop Me's in the street are seen
   Refusing penny ices,

When income tax has rudely wrecked
 Once opulent conditions,
And we meet persons who collect
 For home and foreign missions,

Ah, then, I think, we shall find out,
 As spending power decreases,
That our best friend, without a doubt,
 The little threepenny piece is.

A RUMOUR

My cousin knows a very cute
Commercial traveller in jute
Who met, up north, a man named Spence,
Who told him in strict confidence
That all those things we used to guess
About the Monster of Loch Ness
Were quite beside the mark. "M.I."
Had now interned a German spy
Who boasted to their very face
Loch Ness had been a Nazi base,
And that long dark shape we had seen
Was just a Nazi submarine.

THE HUSH-HUSH PERIOD

No longer every railway station
 Its name in letters large displays:
This very useful information
 Must be acquired in harder ways.

58

The porter with the beery nose is
  A sign the train has stopped at Blank:
Y is announced by scent of roses,
  X by a rusty water-tank.

I change at Dash: it's very simple:
  The nameless seats are painted white;
And where the tea-girl sports a dimple,
  I jump up quickly and alight.

THE ANDERSON SHELTER

We must be resigned
To take shelter in tins:
Though hardly refined,
We must be resigned.
Like sardines streamlined,
Pressed close, for our sins,
We must be resigned
To take refuge in tins.

COST OF LIVING INDEX

Tell me not, in graphed statistics,
  Rising costs are but a dream:
Food stores don't encourage mystics:
  Prices are just what they seem.

Jam is dearer! Ham needs earning!
  And we know the price of sole!
Woolton's maxima, we're learning,
  Aren't adapted to the dole.

Lives of poor men all remind us
   Index costs aren't worth a dime,
And our shopping trips still find us
   Pennies poorer every time.

A GOURMAND INTERVIEWED

'You want my views on war-time grub?
   Well, I'm the chap the Press denounces:
I make sad sounds for bygone pounds
   Reduced by war to mere half-ounces."

"Where is the muffin's butter now?
   The breakfast bacon's ample slices?
That juicy joint which used to point
   Sad morals to our pleasant vices?"

"The law won't let us gormandize:
   The rich no easier than the poor may;
So, if my views are front-page news,
   Quote me as saying, I'm a gourmet."

A BENISON ON WAR-TIME HIGH TEA

Upon this scanty meal, O Lord,
We ask a blessing in accord:
Pour Thy grace in measure small
Lest it more than cover all.

Bless the tiny piece of ham:
Bless the lonely dab of jam:
Bless the sparsely-buttered toast,
Father, Son, and Holy Ghost.

ORANGES FROM SPAIN

The war depression lightly lifts:
  A moment's pleasure physics pain:
Once more the doughty docker shifts
  The golden fruit of sunny Spain.

Crate after crate is swung ashore,
  Manna from bluer, brighter skies;
No Spanish galleon ever bore
  A richer or more welcome prize.

Like some dry stream-bed, freshet-filled,
  Or fountain stopped, that plays again,
In eager mouths is sweetly spilled
  The golden juice of sunny Spain.

DELIGHT IN DISORDER
(After Herrick)

To-day's disorder in the dress
Kindles in me a kindliness:
A City knight in dressing-gown
Searching in Bond Street up and down;
A string-patched lace, and here and there
Socks which would hardly make a pair;
A leg short-trousered, and thereby
Spats out of place amusingly;
A wrinkle grave the world may note
In the smart M.P.'s morning coat;
A ski-boot wearer, in whose tie
I see scholastic vanity;
Do more to touch my war-worn heart
Than when, unbombed, such men were smart.

THE HOME FRONT

Is the cellar you see here to let, sir?
Why, no, sir, it isn't: that's flat!
If I may be so bold,
You could offer me gold,
And I'd just snap my fingers—like that!

It's dark and it's damp, did you say, sir?
That's true, sir; but isn't it strong!
And it's Safety First Hall
When the bombs start to fall,
So I sleep there myself, sir. So long!

O, MISTRESS PORTER!

O, Mistress Porter, how do you do?
I wanted a sort of Samson, but
I'm now engaging you.
Take these two portmanteaux
As quickly as you can:
O, Mistress Porter, don't you wish you were a man?

O, Mistress Porter, where are we now?
Your voice is a lot too ladylike:
Why don't you make more row?
Amplify your larynx
As quickly as you can:
O, Mistress Porter, don't you wish you were a man?

LINES TO GOERING

To you, stout champion of the pure in heart,
The world of beauty owes a second start:

Fair Prussia, rescued from the Jewish maw,
Now finds that genius is the fruit of law;
And painted canvas and strong sculptured stone
Blossom with morals modelled on your own.
Banished the obstinate, degenerate fools
Who railed at discipline and spat at rules:
The cankered chaos of their slime-fed art
Stinks in the sewer of some foreign mart,
While Prussian youth, inspired by thoughts of you,
Create the universe of art anew!

THE LONDON LIBRARY 1841–1941

Here is a library, with learning stored,
Wherein chance flappers are quite frankly bored.
Since eighteen-forty-one its spartan note
Has always got the common reader's goat
By turning down with faint contemptuous grins
A solid century of Godfrey Winns;
No library in London lets in fewer
Cheap choices of the popular reviewer.
Here culture's flag's defiantly unfurled
In welcome only to the thinking world;
And always, if rude bombing planes shall roar,
There'll be a man to show the brutes the door.

A TOTALITARIAN DECALOGUE

1. Thou shalt not worship any God
   Who disobeys the Leader's nod.

2. Give thou no room to works of art
   In which the Hebrew has a part.

3. Swear no great oaths by God on high:
   They rarely reinforce the lie.

4. Keep Sunday holy: it's confessed
   Slaves work the better for a rest.

5. Honour thy parents, but be curst
   If they, and not the State, come first.

6. Thou shalt not kill: that is to say,
   Unless there be no cheaper way.

7. If need be, thou shalt copulate
   Producing bastards for the State.

8. Thou shalt not steal, but may'st arrange
   By legal process forced exchange.

9. Bear secret witness, false or true,
   To what thy neighbours say and do.

10. Thou shalt not covet speech that's free:
    The Leader's there to speak for thee.

FINLAND

(*March*, 1940)

Now God forgive these foolish Finns
   Who lack the wiser patience
To suffer what they call the sins
   Committed by great nations;
Who spill their patriotic blood
In snowy marsh and frozen mud,
Trying, in vain, to stem the flood
   Of new Empire relations.

64

Fate and the hand of time have furled
  The flags of little places:
There is no room in this new world
  For unimportant races;
And Finland's most unwisely bold
To strive against the Russian hold,
When bigger countries, bought and sold,
  Jog humbly in the traces.

Let simple Finns try once again
  To save the situation
And spare the Soviets the pain
  Of bloody liquidation:
Four million people, after all,
Can't hold world tendencies in thrall:
Let them instead help to instal
  A Red civilization.

DISGUST OF COLONEL BLIMP

As Colonel Blimp surveys this war
  With eyeballs popping out,
He certainly has reason for
  Unphilosophic doubt.

With leaflets we began the strife
  And radio backchat:
The gory work of taking life
  Has been held up for that.

And now the Colonel's forced to con
  Another stunt, by Gad!
The Finns are dropping Bibles on
  The Reds of Leningrad.

THE BELLS OF BREDON

(After A. E. Housman)

In war-time now on Bredon,
　　Where bells once sounded clear,
The shires no longer ring them
　　In steeples far and near
　　For happy folk to hear.

If church bells ring this summer
　　It will not be to pray:
'Twill be a call to people
　　To arm them for the fray
　　And keep the foe away.

O, ring no bells on Bredon
　　And let no steeples hum
Until a happy people
　　To pray in church shall come:
　　Till then, O bells, be dumb.

SONG OF WELCOME TO THE NEW SPRING

The silvery, cone-shaped shells peep out
　　Where merryhammers ring;
Comes far and faint the droning plaint
　　Of warplanes on the wing.

In sweet array the cylinders
　　Of mustard vapours lie,
Conveying scent and ravishment
　　To gas-masks fluttering by.

66

Now flaunts the dreadnought on the sea,
    A poem, grey on green;
And here and there comes up for air
    The shrinking submarine.

The clumsy tank sprawls o'er the brown:
    Tall bayonets gleam white:
Here with the dawn to life is born
    The sleeping dynamite.

O, welcome, messengers of Mars,
    To whom our great ones sing!
In you we greet the flying feet
    Of Death's bright crimson spring.

CHINESE ART AT BURLINGTON HOUSE (1935)

With blood our Western glories reek,
    In witless warfare spilt:
Our heroes are the men who wreak
Mass vengeance on the poor and weak,
    Burning where others built.

But old world China always knew
    Arms as a low-class trade:
The mandarin with button blue
Preferred the deeds that craftsmen do
    In ivory and jade.

Through centuries of weal and woe
    The thread of beauty ran;
And artists saw their colours glow
And knew the joy that artists know:
    The deepest known to man.

The ancient craftsmen make no more
    Picture and fan and bowl:
Lost is the magic-fingered lore
That lays, in treasure, on our shore
    China's embalméd soul.

And we, of modern progress proud,
    Savour the lovely things,
And hardly dare to speak aloud,
But pass with heads in homage bowed
    Where bloom of beauty clings . . .

When we have dwelt a million days,
    Ghosts in the hollow vast,
Shall our posterity at gaze
Find glories parallel to praise,
    Or ruins, poison-gassed?

VI
NONSENSE

DARKNESS AND NO DAWN

The binnacle sang in a glittering curve,
  (O Mountain of Burning Soap!)
And there rose and fell like a banished bell
Sweet flowers from the rosy deeps of hell,
  For while there is life there's hope.

Strange whispering grew on a gold-leaf vine,
  (O Freedom of Leadless Glaze!)
For the tale was old, how the darkness cold
Was robbed of its crystal bars of gold
  By knights of the dull dog-days.

The meaning of this is isosceles,
  (O Sacred Syrup of Figs!);
'Tis the ancient plan of the Spick and Span,
So eloquent still of the frying pan
  And the passion for poisoned pigs.

And ye who shall hear of this violent faith,
  (O Rose of the Widowed Pool!);
While your flying feet in soft circles beat,
And the square in horror forsakes its meat,
  Drink *then* of your Gooseberry Fool!

THE TIPPER'S TRAIL

(By Pined Cur-Mission of Spannon Cooner)

Hairless and cappy, along on my sips,
I asked for a word to Thest Kerry:
    The shark, with a clout,
    Tooled the picket right out,
With a fawning: "Go nude on the wherry!"

I found a syce neat in the track of the bane,
Whipped my Scind for a mile in the Deanery;
    Then, beading a rook
    In the nosiest cook,
I bared not a kit for the greenery.

We whopped for a stile at an outspying lot,
To let the town drain pun on Rastus,
    Passing Rye with a bore,
    A tanking, it swore,
With a why from the crystal to blast us.

The guard flopped his drag and the wain got a tray:
The nun-tree was cow-looking, dreary:
    I bade myself lack,
    Fell a-creep in a slack,
And faked wheeling all-wired and teary.

A BISHOP, A BELISHA BEACON, A GIRAFFE, AND A ROADHOUSE

The Bishop, an innocent, meek 'un,
To a roadhouse was lured by a she-con.,
    And ending up tight,
    Saw giraffes in the night,
Drawing beer from a Belisha Beacon.

EXCELSIOR AND CASABIANCA: AN AMALGAMATED VERSION

The flames flashed round the lifeless deck
    And lit the falling mast:
The roaring torrent caught the wreck:
    The wreathing fires rolled past.

And there on high, in splendour wild,
    Shone like a silver star
A burning youth, an Alpine child,
    Who shouted from afar.

His brow was sad with brave despair;
    A tear stood in his eye:
The flames rolled through his waving hair
    Like banners in the sky.

His accents like a clarion rung:
    "Excelsior!' he cried:
Unconscious of that unknown tongue,
    "O stay!" the maiden sighed.

73

Below, his father, faint in death,
    Chanted the pious prayer:
"Beware the booming glacier's breath!
    Beware the cold night air!"

"Try not the snow," the old man said,
    "When household fires gleam bright!"
The breath of life had all but fled:
    This was his last good-night.

But still, heroic, stood his son,
    Half-buried in the storm,
"Excelsior!" his lips upon,
    Flames on his spectral form.

Again his voice at break of day
    Streamed on the air around:
"Excelsior! Father, must I stay?"
    —There came a thunder-sound!

The mast and helm and pennon fair
    Were strewed upon the sea;
But heavenward through the startled air
    The boy—O, was that he?

And in the sky was heard once more,
    Faint from that gallant heart,
The clarion word: "Excelsior!"
    That well had borne its part.

THE AGNOSTIC

All ears, he stared at the receding night
And felt the dim pulsations of the light.
The wistful day hung out its clothes to dry
As naked epigrams, ashamed, slunk by
To catch the boat for Wigan. Far and near
The blended carrot sighed and changed its gear . . .

Could these things be? Was Truth, then, like a cow
That barked in simple wantonness, or how?
His square-cut cheeks grew faint; at last he knew
The utter oiliness of pea-fed glue!
In curled despair his idle whiskers fled,
Nor could he hear the weary words they said.

But suddenly his long and piercing nose
Swung round most graciously and soothed his toes
With muted music, while the weeping sun
Spoke kindly to him, like a braised Bath bun . . .
And so he died, nor ever was he known
From thence, to trim his toe-nails with a hone.

UTTER ABANDON

She loved him! How her ankle throbbed to know
Her chin was his, and hers his tiniest toe!
With simple subtlety she blamed her youth
Whose every fond, impressionable tooth
Leapt out to meet him. O, 'twas hard to feel
That straying dimples must be brought to heel

And all her cracking joints cemented firm
In cool restraint—she who so loved to squirm,
Voiceless but happy, in his hand! Yet once
Her far-flung passion choked its bleeding bonds:
Her beauty *should* be seen! (The author's blush
Here checks the even tenour of this slush.)
With trembling hair and elbows all on fire
She lit the glowing current of desire:
"My love, behold!" she cried, and flaming there
In splendid shame she laid her eyebrows bare.

GARDEN PARTY

His eyes were bright: his vest was white; his shoes were
    tied with twine:
His silk top-hat and single spat were glistening with
    brine;
And on the tick, not span but spick, he turned up brisk
    and hearty
To greet with playful, twice-cocked snooks, the hostess
    of the party.

She gave him ham: she gave him jam: she brought him
    pots of tea;
But he was proud and cried aloud: "These will not do
    for me!
Bring basic tar; bring caviar!" She said: "I beg your
    pardon:
Those are not quite the sort of things one thinks of in a
    garden."

The other guests—a crowd of pests!—buzzed round
  and gave him beans:
They plainly thunk that he was drunk and fond of
  making scenes;
But with a start (dramatic art!) he cried in accents hearty:
"God bless me, do you mean to say this is a *garden*
  party?"

NIGHTMARE

He pressed me closer to the wall,
a fearsome creature, gaunt and tall,
tied coils of tape about my nape
and squeezed my body like a grape;
then with an unstamped envelope
he gagged the very door of hope!
I heard him shout: "Your luck is out!
Stalin prescribes the naughty knout,
red lipstick, racks and beauty packs
for those who balk at income-tax!"
The words he spoke became a croak
and, heaven be thanked, at last I woke.

VII
PARODIES AND IMITATIONS

B*rn*rd Sh*w.

THE OPENING PARAGRAPH OF G. B. S.'s MEMOIRS

If anyone expects that the book about to be inflicted on her is the usual farrago of anecdote and inanity, faulty recollection and stale wit, which goes by the name of Memoirs, she is, I am afraid, wholly justified. In me the exuberance of youth has given place to the garrulity of age: what message I had to deliver I have repeated to the point of nausea: nothing remains for me now but the saltless hack-writing of the book maker. But I protest that I am not to blame. What man in my position, or in any position, could have the heart to reject an offer of a million pounds sterling (free of tax) for a single book? This is the breath-bereaving offer of the Amalgamated British and American Publishers, Inc., for the thin dregs of my genius's nectar. The offer, coming on top of the Greater War's disillusions, has been too much for me: I have succumbed.

But do not despair. I daresay I can vamp up enough literary virtuosity, even at ninety, to persuade you that what you are reading is something dazzlingly new and important, though I must go on saying, whether you listen or not, that it is nothing of the kind . . .

W*lt*r R*l**gh.*

TASTES OF A NOT SO ELDERLY MAN

I rather like the Science Race;
I rather like its prudent pace;
I love its friendly human talks;
I love its blackboards and its chalks;
But what I fancy most of all
Is sound of new words as they fall;
And when I heard the latest one
I cried aloud: *What jolly Phon!*

J*hn M*s*f**ld.

A BRIEF BOUT OF LAND FEVER

I must go back to the land again,
    to the homely plough till I die,
To the brave smell of the brown earth
    that makes my heart beat high;
And all I ask is a soft rain
    on the green crops falling,
And the dogs' bark and the lambs' bleat
    and the curlews calling.

J*hn M*s*f**ld.

KING ALFRED AND THE CAKES

"By Christ, His Blood, a narrow shave,"
Gasped Alfred as he flung his stave
Down on the floor, and took his rest
A sorry, uninvited guest,
Beside the good old woman's fire,
And piled her Silkstone Cobbles higher.

"And now there's nought to do but think,
(O, Lord, I wish I had a drink!):
What was it that old woman said?
Oh, yes, she said she'd clout my head
If I forgot her silly cakes
And let 'em burn. Forget! . . . Good sakes!
Can I forget the bloody ground
Where brains and guts were scattered round
Making a ghastly, gory muck! . . .
There never was such rotten luck!"
He thought of Bruce and his old spider:
It made him dry: he'd like some cider.
This woman's hut was hot as Hell . . .
Outside the great wind rose and fell,
The thunder rumbled to a crash,
The rain descended like a lash:
"If God's in's heaven," (his simple thought)
"He's acting like he didn't ought!"
Then through the storm's infernal mood
He heard the old girl chopping wood,
And when the thunder ceased to linger,
He heard her swear: she'd chipped her finger.
"This peasant's life's all smoke and smother,
And chopping this and chipping t'other;
If I should live," said Alf. "this hell
I'll change . . . But what a blarsted smell!"
The lightning flickered through the winders
And Alfred saw the cakes in cinders.
His heavy spirit dropped like lead:
"That woman said she'd clout my head,
And if she does, the thing's undoubted,
The head of England's king is clouted!"
And he was dropping off agen

To introspective musings, when
She entered and began on him:

"You idle, graceless, feckless limb!
You sneaking, snivelling, stinking stoat!
I'll ram them cinders down your throat!
Ochone, to burn my bits o' buns,
I'd like to see you blown from guns!
Those cakes were baked with finest flour,
As white as the pale lilyflower
That stars with light our English mead;
Out of my bitter, bitter need
I kneaded them: their thought did loose
The palate's psychologic juice . . .
And now they're burnt and the cold moon
Looks down on yon God-damnéd loon!"
"Peace, woman," Alf. at length spoke out:
"For God's sake, give my head a clout,
Then hold your noise. In Billingsgate
Was never poured so coarse a spate."

The legend spares the royal head
And Alf. went presently to bed.
When times were better, so 'tis told,
Alf. sent the woman, done in gold,
A griddle new, a late invention,
That worked without a king's attention.

L*g*n P**rs*ll Sm*th.

SPOTS ON SPRING

When cheerful idiots of my acquaintance tell me all
over again what spring does to a young man's fancy, I
am impelled to reply impatiently: "It also turns his face

to spots." And that's the rub! For most of spring's eruptions I have all a poet's passion. Bursting buds delight me; early morning dew and green, thrusting grass—these are charming; bursts of song from bird or poet—good! But I bar the facial spots of spring. Like the late Lord Rosebery, I appreciate manly men and womenly women; but I hate a boily boy.

D*m*n R*ny*n.

ON HENRY JAMES

If Henry James ever keeps a speak, I am not one of his customers. I am a guy that reads more than somewhat, but Henry's merchandise is harder to take in than Good Time Charley's. And that is more than talking. Indeed, if I see one of Henry's tales coming, I haul off and walk away, because he is a guy from whom I get no literary scratch. I never give the large hello to the guys and dolls in his pieces. They have too much tongue, and however long they snow, I am not getting their drift, so what is the use of going around with them? I will only wish to poke them in the smush. There is a writing guy that says Henry is like a hippopotamus picking up a pea. That seems right to me. Let him get on with it. But me, I am no piker. I like to run around with simple, tough guys that have a guy's slant on dolls and guys. I do not care to see a guy all tangled up in his mind over a thin dime. I get sored up. So that is how Henry strikes me. I do not mind playing the chill on him like this, because he never packs a Betsy, and even if I try to cool him off he will just argue with me till I am daffy. Also he dies quite a while back. But I still wish he is never born.

SOME WELL-KNOWN CHARACTERS DISCUSS CHEAP BOOKS

LADY BRACKNELL. Prism! What are you trying to conceal from me in that handbag?

MISS PRISM. Indeed, Lady Bracknell, it is only one of the new sixpennies. A Penguin.

LADY BRACKNELL. The zoological significance of the smaller coinage at the moment escapes me. Pray explain yourself.

LORD HENRY WOTTON. Miss Prism refers to the issue, for popular consumption of paper-backed volumes, foolishly named "Penguins," and sold at the cheap rate of sixpence each. You will agree, Lady Bracknell, that there is only one thing in the world worse than paying sixpence for a book.

LADY BRACKNELL. And that is?

LORD HENRY. Having to pay seven-and-sixpence.

LADY BRACKNELL. I do not buy books, Lord Henry. I am aware that society demands that certain books must be read, but I see no reason to pamper the authors by purchasing them. Prism, what is the book about?

MISS PRISM. Incredible though it may seem, Lady Bracknell, the work appears to deal with your private affairs and mine. Lord Henry, I think, is not referred to.

LORD HENRY (*languidly*). I should hope not. No man in my position can afford to have his private affairs exposed to the vulgarity of linotype and half-inch margins.

LADY BRACKNELL. I cannot agree. There are worse things than being written about, even in the sixpennies. One might easily not be written about at all. Prism: where did you obtain this—ah—Penguin?

Miss Prism. At Victoria Station, Lady Bracknell.

Lady Bracknell. Ah, indeed! Your associations with London's larger termini have not been invariably so happy. You will give me the book, Prism. Pray buy yourself another copy.

J*m*s J*yc*.

JAMES JOYCE RE-WRITES A PASSAGE FROM PROUST

(*The passage chosen is from "*Sodome et Gomorrhe.*" It describes the reaction of Proust's own servants, Céleste Albaret and her sister Marie Gineste, to one of their master's foibles—his insistence on eating in bed without using a table-napkin.*)

It's she had the passon for similichoobs volpinched from the animazoo. The deer nose he don't clothe his eyes atoll atoll, she would murmut. Flutterbutter he flies in the nighty, and daydawn he's a three squir'l for the jumpabout—a thatzimthatwoz, the sort that goes flicker-wik in the old shaynoo till it has the glimpies of ye fair batblinded. Ah now, but why will ye be for ever bibantuckering the poor lamb that likes to manchew his frugrunch all purthy-durthy? Arrahgwan, it's he doesn't mind tuckuppin his nappequin like a lillord fauntletory. The ould dictitler av him only crumsples the bedlamin fr'm hindmighty motovs. Ten daily Times ye can nurswitch the great white cheefts of his leiderdown, an they dinmarked, but such is the grimmage an spitery of the ould pissanpan he'll dribbledrop 'em agenanagen . . . Sure, I spake wid the tungalungs of marxn engels when I towelld ye the great god Nevvn niver intended the masther to be pinnyless.

87

J. B. M*rt*n (B**chc*mb*r).

A FILL-UP

MYSELF (*reciting*).

In Quito, where the half-spheres meet,
There's nothing much except the heat:
Once in five years they get a breeze,
And then the grateful people sneeze.

PRODNOSE. What is this nonsense? Quito gets plenty breezes.

MYSELF (*patiently*). Shut up, hog.

PRODNOSE. Oh, well, if that's what you call poetic licence, I've nothing more to say.

MYSELF. Thank God for that. Now I can get the other one off my chest:

Aunt Jane once kept this dear old cow
Behind her motor car in tow;
But though the darling ran like Hell,
It couldn't give her milk as well.

PRODNOSE. Well, I must say!

MYSELF. Not at all.

Anth*n* Tr*ll*p*.

A PASSAGE OMITTED FROM "BARCHESTER TOWERS"

(*The imagined passage is inserted after the words : " Sixty thousand broad sheets dispersing themselves daily among his (Mr. Slope's) reading fellow-citizens, formed in his eyes a better depot for supremacy than a throne at Windsor, a Cabinet in Downing Street, or even an assembly at Westminster. And on this subject we must not quarrel with Mr. Slope, for the feeling is too general to be met with disrespect.*"

He would, indeed, have preferred the sixty thousand to be six hundred thousand, or six millions. To have the ear of the multitude, to be in a position to impress the incomparable merits of Mr. Slope on an entire nation in a single article, or better still, a single speech, would be a triumph indeed. And, though not as a rule given to day-dreaming, he allowed himself to dally for a few moments with the idea of some ingenious extension of the electric telegraph, by means of which he, Obadiah Slope, might charm England's myriads with one masterly oratorical effort. He saw himself standing beside the magical instrument, while a deferential chairman introduced him in honeyed words: "Ladies and gentlemen of England, the name of Obadiah Slope may not as yet be known to all of you, but soon it will be heard wherever there is talk of piety, eloquence, and erudition. Young in years, Mr. Slope is old in the knowledge of good and in the wisdom of righteousness. To-night the nation is to benefit by those gifts of unmatched oratory which so far have been the treasured privilege of a few. Ladies and gentlemen, Mr. Slope!"

It did occur to Mr. Slope that if such facilities existed, he himself would hardly be the only one to enjoy them; but this disturbing possibility did no more than vouchsafe him a further vision of personal triumph. England now obediently hearkened while he engaged Mr. Arabin in theological controversy. Emerging victorious over a humiliated opponent, he pleased everyone by generously over-praising Mr. Arabin's courage. Tom Towers's letter, which he still held, recalled to the Bishop's chaplain that his present hope was not of a nation eating out of his hand, but the more moderate triumph of the deanship of Barchester . . .

Ch*rl*s K*ngsl*y.

DRY UP, SWEED DOSE!

By streaming dose, I have do sog to sig you:
Do dote you'd hear 'while sdeezes have their way;
Bud, if I cad, wud wistful straid I'll brig you
    This paidful day.

Dry up, sweed dose, ad led whad bust grow redder:
Breathe lovely air, dot stob id all day log;
Ad so bake sbell ad breath do foul gerb-spreader,
    Bud pure ad strog!

Edw*rd F*tzg*r*ld.

OMAR ON A GRAND NATIONAL COMMENTARY

  There was a Voice from which I dared not flee:
There was a Roaring like a Troubled Sea:
    Some raucous shouts awhile of Four to Three
I heard—and then the Voice recaptured Me.

  Awake! it cried, for yonder once again
The seed of Old Kahilan spurns the Plain;
    And lo! in Paradise, with quivering limbs,
The Mare of the Old Woman shares the Strain.

  Now shook the Voice, confusing Speech and Speed,
As though the Stentor were himself the Steed:
    Each Leap that brought the Victor nearer Goal
The Man unseated who but told the Deed.

*   *   *   *

I sometimes think that never grew the Hair
Kept on by Commentators of the Air;
    That every Broadcast from a Field of Sport
Takes off a Tuft the Voice can hardly spare.

L*w*s C*rr*ll.

ON MODERN NOISES

" You are old, Father William," the young man said:
" Your sleep should demand peace and quiet,
Yet you slumber when road-drills awaken the dead:
Pray what's your prescription? I'll try it."

"My wife," Father William replied to his son,
"Used to yap every night like a cur;
And the noise of a road-drill has hardly begun
Ere I'm sleeping and dreaming of her."

"You were not, Father William, when you were a lad,
Case-hardened to siren and horn,
And since no modern racket has driven *you* mad,
Can you tell me why *my* nerves are torn?"

"You've been brought up too kindly," his father replied,
"Your weaknesses clamour for tears:
One treatment, however, remains to be tried,"—
And he thoroughly clouted both ears.

FRAGMENT FROM AN ODE TO A BELISHA BEACON:

"That it be cast down"

Glass orange of odious yellow:
　　Pale spouse of the polychrome pole:
Make the most of thy honeymoon mellow,
　　Ere sinister swells spill thy soul!
Thy death-dealers dilly and dally,
　　But hate in their hearts groweth green,
And thou art too plain an Aunt Sally
　　To save thy bald bean.

Beware! Thou art brazen but brittle,
　　And loomest a luminous mass . . .
Hast thou heard of the sport of the skittle?
　　Canst thou dodge as the deadly things pass?
Soon motorists madly may maul thee,
　　Pedestrians prance on thy plot,
Till not even coppers can call thee
　　To life " on the spot."

L*rd M*c**l*y.

EXTRACT FROM THE NEW HORATIUS

When the four-ale bar is crowded,
　　and a score of gaspers lit,
When the latest from Newmarket makes
　　the rude old cabmen spit;
When the wireless tea-time music, by request,
　　turns faint and goes;
And a dozen grumpy voices murmur:
　　"Damn all radios!"

92

When the bookie counts his winnings
  and looks out for mugs to trim;
When the loafer dreams of doubles
  and all they mean to him—
Then the boozer tells the barmaid,
  who quite forgets to flirt,
How Richards stole Fred Archer's cloak
  and saved the punter's shirt!

R*dy*rd K*pl*ng.

THE DOWDY MOTORIST

*(The President of the Merchant Taylors' Company thinks the
modern motorist is badly dressed.)*

If you can doff that greasy mackintosh,
  And cease to buy your lounge suits off the peg;
If you can send more collars to the wash,
  Wear smarter ties and keep them free from egg;
If you can pull up socks that never jar
  And swap that hat for any decent one—
Why then, you'll be a model, like your car;
  What's more: you'll miss the Taylors' ban, my son!

R. B. Sh*r*d*n.

MRS. MALAPROP ON SPELLING BEES

"La, Sir Anthony, there is nothing more collusive to
a proper depreciation of orthodoxy than a well-deranged
spelling-bee. I myself was always incessantly fond of
such eremite conjugations when I was under titillary
distraint. I would apprehend the most extenuating words

93

and spell them out syllabub by syllabub, till 'twas feared such easy felicity was almost auspicious in one so young. Oh, I assure you, Sir Anthony, without exacerbation, that I was quite in my aliment where spelling-bees were discerned. I am certain my posteriors will never rise to such incredulous heights of deficiency."

J*n*th*n Sw*ft.

A VOYAGE TO CYNOSURIA

(*A land populated by intelligent dogs*)

. . . When I was recovered of my well-deserved biting, my master, that placid and dignified St. Bernard, promised me that if I behaved well and showed myself docile and of clean house habits, he would presently enlarge me from the kennel where I lay into the freedom of his own dwelling. "For," said he (and by now I began to comprehend the Wowff speech very well) "though you Lacktails are puppishly conceited and quarrelsome, you are not without a measure of intelligence, when suitably encouraged."

In halting and humble speech, I thanked him, promising in return for his kindness to a miserable two-footed animal that I would try to emulate my master in all things, such as making a better use of my nose than blowing it, endeavouring to walk like a rational being on four legs, and praying (since my unaided efforts were of no avail) for hair to cover my nakedness and a tail to lend me dignity.

I fear, however, from the look in my master's eye, that this speech only confirmed him in his belief in my conceit. None the less, he kept his word, and in about a fortnight, he gave me the run of his own well-appointed

94

mansion, where I soon became the inseparable pet of his housemaid, a jolly, spotted Dalmatian. She liked nothing better than to roll me over on my back and tickle my belly with her cool nose till I wriggled with pleasure. I was fed on the juiciest and tenderest bones, and a special hearth rug was tacitly appropriated to my exclusive use. Here I would lie while Dalmatia was busy with the house-work and (somewhat ungratefully) dream of the England I would never see again.

R*b*rt H*rr*ck.

TO JULIA, NOT TO USE COSMETICKS

> If ye will with me find grace,
> Never show a raddled face:
> Even Julia's lips Ile miss
> Leave they Stain at ev'ry Kiss.
> Ape not sluts in poudre veil'd,
> Henna-hair'd and Ruby nail'd:
> Love himself would bend no bow
> Did he spy my Julia so.

Sh*k*sp**r.

W.S. PENS A WEATHER FORECAST

So please you, sirs, the weather will be fine
And something warmer, but with frost at night:
Upon the sea, a north-east wind shall whip
The sullen waves to half-reluctant play,
And bird-men, weaving patterns in the sky,
Shall feel the breeze. What still may hap's in doubt.

AN ELIZABETHAN ANTI-VICE SOCIETY PROTESTS AFTER THE FIRST PERFORMANCE OF ROMEO AND JULIET

". . . in particular, the bawd, Mercutio. Marry come up! Shall our simple maids be debauched by the lewd intent of a tinsel-gilt, rascally rakehell, a paltry playhouse pimp, whose empty mind is but a thirsty conduit for a loose scribbler's filth? Go to, sirs, is not fornication rife enow among us that ye must instruct the very prentices that goggle, ears-a-twitch, from the back benches, to look with lecherous eye upon their masters' maids? Ay, marry, and ye think to cozen wiser heads with a honey of the sweet-sounding words Master Shakespear hath ever at his call. Yet are they in truth but the rainbow scum that masks the stinking waters of iniquity. Content ye, sirs, ye cannot long pull wool over honest eyes.

Now hearken. This our company, full formed of sober citizens and matrons well reputed, demands of you that ere this Tragedy be further shown, Mercutio's part shall wholly be excised. Ay so! And let the speeches of the rest be strictly scoured and sweetened till they fit the gentle ear. Attune them to this gracious, holy time, made good by Great Elizabeth, our virtuous, virgin Queen, whom God preserve!

This night, some part of our good company shall look again upon your players' art. See to it that the tale be such as brings no blush to maiden cheek, nor draws unseemly approbation forth from idle fools—lewd fellows of the baser sort.

And so, God be with you."

GOERING ADDRESSES THE TAILORS

Pale slaves, whose scissors hold some magic charm
To trim with majesty the human form,
Give ear! We would that presently you cut
For this our eager body such a suit
As we may fitly wear to hunt the Jew.
Nay, stir not yet. Our soul hath richer thirsts.
Ye must contrive a doublet, blue and gold,
To overawe the cits; and one of hue
More sober, clothed wherein we shall rebuke
The stiff-necked pastors who still prate of God.
Unroll your stuffs and spread them on the floor:
Our mind on uniforms runs more and more.

THIS RAILWAY STATION

This squalid dome of soot-obscuréd glass,
This larger lavatory or spittoon,
This vault of echoes, rudely amplified,
This meeting-place of draughts, whose smut-filled air
Strikes chill upon the stoutest traveller's chest,
This worried trippers' haunt, this dunghill world
Whence porter-cocks crow false civilities,
This traffic jam, stirred in a thousand jars,
Which serves as hypodermic for the times,
Inoculating tourists 'gainst the press
Of progress and the piercing shrieks of speed,
This dark and dank depression of the soul,
This builder's blot, this curse, this Railway Station.

VIII
MISCELLANEOUS VERSE

WHAT'S IN A NAME?

A Ballad from the Telephone Directory [1]

From Beaglehole to Yallop town
   The Laughland lay in flood;
And many a steer from Godbehere
Was driven mad by panic fear
   And perished in the mud.

The wires were down on Godsave Hill;
   And near the Halfhead mark
The wild wind's whip on Teago Stripp
Had flogged a little sailing-ship
   To death on Deadman Dark.

From Killingbeck to Littleales,
   Along the Cursue bank,
The living leaves fell thick as thieves
And corn came floating down in sheaves
   And in the shallows sank.

All Twaddle men, and Greater Gloak,
   From Cannot down to Thing,
Remained that day within to pray,
And far-off folk, Whalebelly way,
   Heard Anguish church-bells ring.

---

[1] The names used, however, are of persons and not, as in the text, of places.

A DRINKING SONG

A man there was, and it is said
He drank fat ale from dawn till bed,
And such a merry life he led,
   With canakins a-clinking!
CHORUS. Come you potman, fill agen:
       Set the froth a-winking!
       Beer was brewed for honest men
       And throats were made for drinking!

Now you might hear this fellow shout:
The country need not fear a drought
Until our inns be running out
   Of beer for good men's drinking.

He never suffered pain or ache
Because he never failed to take
Strong liquor for his stomach's sake,
   A fact there is no blinking!

And there was wisdom in his plan
To drown all sorrows in the can,
For thus he lengthened his life's span
   And saved a lot of thinking.

When beer grew weak, he did not thrive:
He passed away at ninety-five,
Though many hold he's still alive
   And only ale is sinking!

THE PROMISED LAND

O Hollywood the golden, with balmy breezes blest,
Where beauty humps the sidewalk in next to nothing
    dressed,
Where hash is slung by Hebes, and soda-jerkers are
Each fired with the ambition to be a movie-star!

I thirst to walk thy gardens, eccentrically planned,
And stand in at thy parties, when all the guests are
    canned:
I pine to enter cafés whose fascinating spells
Are exercised by looking so much like something else.

Thy studios, how gorgeous! where Limey authors,
    penned,
In well-paid, silent boredom, the rare brainwave attend;
Where art-inspired directors make purple passions bleed,
And half-a-million dollars is so much chicken feed!

O Hollywood the golden, with grape-fruit flowing free,
When shall thy Bowl enormous be scrambled in by me?
When shall I see on scooters, O boy! O Boy! O Boy!
Clark Gable, Greta Garbo and maybe Myrna Loy?

PELION ON OSSA

(A Sonnet in Journalese)

Stark tragedy has reared its ugly head
Above the hallowed quiet of this town;
For, shrouded in her blood-bespattered gown,
A victim of the craze for speed lies dead.

The impact of a shining four-wheeled Death,
A ton of steel hurled headlong through the air,
Has made a mangled corpse of what was fair,
And in the broken body quenched the breath.

Somewhere in London, speaking through the 'phone,
A blasé editor receives the news,
Tapping a small lead pencil on his knees:
"You'll find out if the woman's name is known?
A picture? Yes, of course. No time to lose.
And, by the way, full mutilations, please!"

LAMENT OF A GEORGIAN

(An exercise in excruciating rhymes)

To us old poets, this new style
    Of obscurantist drooling
Is water in the Muses' oil,
    Unspiritual fuelling.

Our Georgian days were not so poor
    In the divine afflatus:
We sipped strong lyrics like liqueur
    And wore the Muses' garters.

Spill out this cheap swipes, thin and sour,
    So unlike honest liquor,
And into singing measures pour
    The poet's genuine ichor.

Drink deep of this, the ancient wine,
   So radiant, so translucent!
And if the Muse should put a dye in,
   Don't tell her that she mustn't.

WHEN SKIES WERE BLUE: 1980 LOOKS BACK

As now I hover in my plane,
   By gyrostat suspended,
I dream of those sweet days again,
   Which with my youth were ended.

I used to see the sky quite clear,
   With scarce a cloud to fleck it;
The lark's ecstatic song I'd hear,
   With no sky-roar to check it.

We always then looked up for peace
   And hardly had a notion
The sky might soon be one great piece
   Of aerial locomotion.

We drove about in little cars:
   (Ah me, my Austin Seven!)
And traffic was a splendid farce,
   And " doing eighty " heaven.

'Tis many, many years since I
   Clung earthbound with those people,
And I would like to see the sky,
   And look *up* at a steeple.

A PETITION AGAINST BORES

From raconteurs who roost in clubs,
and spouting demagogues on tubs;
from chaps who clutch our buttonholes
to tell us things about their souls;
from breakfast jokers, giggling maids,
from hobby-horsemen of all grades;
from snub-nosed infants, far from shy,
who never tire of asking: Why?
from women, restless as the midge,
who want us for a fourth at bridge;
from bores too painful to discuss,
we pray: Good Lord, deliver us!

SOME PERSONAL AMBITIONS

It is my ambition
to make sedition
if not undetectable,
then respectable.

I desire to invent
a sort of Totalitarian scent
which would attract dictators
to bottomless craters.

I would love
to live long enough
to read, with proper awe,
the Complete Letters of Bernard Shaw.

When I die, I want
to haunt,
on suitable dates,
all Waits.

MY LAST WILL AND TESTAMENT

... My winnings in the Penny Pool
I leave to found a Betting School;
this Brewery Stock's for Shaw to take
for candles on his birthday cake;
five pounds to E. C. Bentley's due
to pay for Trent's First Clerihew;
a crate (3 doz.) of nettle beer
I give to Belloc—O, and here
for General Streicher to peruse
Is Milman's "History of the Jews."
My Old Moore's Almanac's for Wells
(first aid in his prophetic spells);
a fruity story of his boss
I leave in trust for Castlerosse,
and Earp, for giving me a prize,
inherits all my Old School Ties.

I REMEMBER ...

I remember, I remember
   The art of long ago!
When "Two Alone", by Marcus Stone,
   Made all our bosoms glow;
When Leighton's " Psyche at the Bath"
   Was "supplement"-ed free,
And ten R.A.'s called cattle home
   Across the Sands of Dee.

The friendly seas now turn their back
And leave but pools of ink, blue-black;
Yon mast that dips and dips again
Is the stark shadow of a pen.
See, ruler-wise, th'horizon place
A line below levanted days.
These sands, once golden in the sun,
Seem plain mahogany for writing on.
The sun himself, no more benign,
Says coldly: "Monday sharp at nine!"

ODE TO AN ELECTRIC MILKING MACHINE

Sweet purrs thy dynamo, mechanic maid,
  A soothing sound to heavy-uddered kine:
Lulled to a drowsy peace, their lowing stayed,
  They wait the throbbing of thy suction line.
Yon lovelorn farm-lad, stricken moveless, cons
  Thy seamless, shining pails of phosphor bronze.

Now thy pulsator's bosom swells with pride:
  A lifting quiver runs through all thy veins:
Thy clenchéd liners ope and shut: the tide
  Of warm new milk thy slender being strains.
Alas, bright maid, that thou canst never know
  The stream of life thy service helps to flow!

THE POLITICIAN TO HIS LOVE

Sweet, shall I always have to clear my throat
And spout the clichés that turn Members blue?
Nor ever hope to sound that higher note
(Ah me!) exploring avenues with you?
Once more to nail my colours to the mast;
To leave no stone unturned, in lonely state?
Not so! I'll turn my back upon the past,
Say what I want and why I will not wait:
Locarno and Geneva, league and pact,
Treaty, alliance, soft soap, world cement:
On these I've lavished loyalty and tact,
Which all for you (I see it now) were meant.
   Come, sweet: what matter though the Whips should
      pout?
   The floor is ours: shall we start walking out?

THE ANGELS OF THE CHAIR

Poets have praised with all their art
Mere orators who owe their start
   To wide jaws, loosely hung,
While men who mend and mould the jaw
Fight poverty with tooth and claw,
   Unhonoured and unsung.

Is there, for architects of gums,
No busy bard to beat the drums
   With fame-arousing roll?
Must men of ivory and gold
Remain for ever in the cold,
   On thrifty honour's dole?

Not so! If Masefield cannot spare
The time to write a passing fair,
　Sweet poem in their praise;
If Tennyson and Browning could
Not understand just why *they* should—
　Then I'll award the bays.

Indeed, it is not hard to feel
Respect for him who clinks the steel
　In water kindly warm,
And with injection of cocaine
Destroys the devil ranks of pain
　Ere they have time to form.

What other man has magic power
To force the aches of hell to cower
　And fly in full retreat?
Who plucks, like him, the rooted woe,
Accepting half-a-crown or so
　For his impressive feat?

Too many of our sorry ills
We owe to hollows, which he fills—
　A heavenly navvy's stunt!
And more than thanks to him are due
For every mouthful that we chew
　In comfort and content.

I see all dentists, clothed in white,
As wingless angels, shining bright
　Behind their golden chairs,
Who, waving magic wands beneath,
Create a world of flashing teeth
　To serve as human spares.

And one day God, who gave them skill
To work the wonders of his will,
　　May lighten dentists' glooms
By sending down the earthly means
To bring to date the magazines
　　In all their waiting-rooms.

THE EXAM.

(*Analytic*)

There's prejudice here:
　　I should have passed high.
That " viva " bloke's sneer?
There's prejudice here!
It seems pretty clear;
　　But say so? My eye!
There's prejudice here:
　　I should have passed high.

(*Apprehensive*)

What am I to say
　　When at home they ask, Why?
The deuce is to pay:
What am I to say?
Not laugh it away:
　　I daren't even try!
What am I to say
　　When at home they ask: Why?

Why should I repine?
   One passes or fails.
Though failure is mine,
Why should I repine?
I'll go out and dine
   With companionate males:
Why should I repine?
   One passes or fails.

A POEM IN HEADLINES

Press Conference Report in Full;
   No More Small Print?
Lord Blank Says Daily Papers Dull;
   All Headlines Hint.

Shaw's Characteristic Quip:
   Why Print At All?
Sees Dailies One Huge Comic Strip:
   Would Pictures Pall?

Our Readers' Views: Opticians Hit;
   More Unemployed?
Makes Centenarian Author Spit;
   Oxford Annoyed.

U.S. Approves; Hearst Cables "Oke";
   Headlining Wins!
Stop Press: Lord Blank Admits Bad Joke;
   Press Peer All Grins.

AN ALPHABET OF BAD MANNERS

A is An Aggressively haughty Attitude
   not even remotely related to a beatitude;

B is a Back-Slapper,
   out of a novel by Sapper;

C is the Cut.
   Not quite the thing: anything but!

D stands for the Dirty Dog
   who is seriously obscene in a smoke-fog;

E might as well be Excesses—
   drink, you know, or, in a poet, too many S's;

F? Oh, Fingering things
   that are someone else's belongings;

G is of course the Grin
   that one wants to stick a pin in;

H is the Hustle Habit:
   you don't say, "Madam, after you": you just grab it;

I is certainly for Interrupter,
   than whom, possibly, no one is corrupter;

J stands for Jilt,
   which implies not merely bad manners but positive
      guilt;

K is the facetious Kidder,
   who (I hope you agree) deserves, not a wife, but a
      widder;

L is a Litter Lout;
   hackneyed, I know, but I daren't leave him out;

M is for Marginalia,
   written in your books by borrowers: words fail ye!

N is for Nagging:
    the only answer to which is sandbagging;

O is dedicated to Ogle
    which isn't nice whether the object be a typist or a
        hello-girl;

P is for Peas eaten with a knife:
    this is bad form, and also what a Cockney would call
        "unsife";

Q is just, well—the Queue
    where I take the opportunity of squeezing in front
        of you;

R is for Rudeness
    which may or may not take the form of lewdness;

S is undoubtedly the Sneer
    an expression no really sound moralist can cheer;

T is to Trump your partner's Tricks
    and be dropped on, very rightly, like a ton of bricks;

U is for Undergrads,
    an abbreviation which naturally annoys the lads;

V is for Vandal
    whose conduct was (and is) generally regarded as a
        scandal;

W's for Wink:
    the high sign of a low-life gink;

X stands for Xenophobe,
    a shockingly unsocial citizen of the globe;

Y is the sort of Yawn
    which sounds like the tootle of a hunting horn;

Z can only be "Zzzzz"—that which causes passengers
        pain
    when whistled through the teeth in a railway train.

SUMMER PASTORAL (Bouts-rimés)

Here in the wood the air is cool:
    Tall tree-guards on parade
With outflung arms contrive a pool
    Of most delightful shade.
Beyond lie fields of golden corn,
    A rolling, sunlit main:
Afar, a mellow, muted horn:
    Murmur of bees in the lane.

THE QUALITY OF QUIET

The quietude that hallows peace
    Is not in perfect stillness found:
The silent times that bring release
    Are saturate with quiet sound.

The whispering zephyr soothes unheard:
    The headlong insect's drowsy hum
Eludes the ear, as though none stirred;
    And even singing birds seem dumb.

Silence is but the sweetest voice
    In nature's many-throated choir:
The spirit's rapt, unconscious choice
    When ruder harmonies would tire.

The jingle sweet of coin unspent
is parsimony's argument:
to stand aside while others give
the vanities that help us live;
to borrow, with a secret leer,
what careless friends have purchased dear;
from niggling huckster's price to pare
the trifle more than honour's share;
to meet expense one cannot check
by salvage from another's wreck;
to sweat, a willing galley-slave,
that one may save, and save, and save;
in bliss all blind to human trace
in saving, of a saving grace;
such joys for meaner souls are meant,
whose thrift leaves even life unspent.

CONSIDER THE LILIES ...

When from the womb of Mother Earth
    The star-eyed flowers are born,
No anxious whisper hints of dearth:
        No heart is torn.

The leaf-green cradles, one by one,
    With dewy darlings fill;
And growing lovelier in the sun
        Is all their will.

They wax not old with weight of cares,
   Nor bend their backs with toil:
What need, when honeydew is theirs
   From air and soil?

Gently they fade, then cease to be,
   Turning to scented dust,
Their lives a brief epitome
   Of blind, wise trust.

SUMMERTIME: AN ACROSTIC

Slow and sweet is the day as the slumber of morning,
Under the snow-dappled blue of the sky in the heat;
Magic the shimmering mists that are rent in the dawning,
Masks of the sun-god, discarded, they melt at my feet.
Even zephyrs at play in the trees hush their laughter,
Relax at their games and all-drowsily dream in the shade;
Time checks the roar of his loom; in the peace that
   comes after,
I hear a faint echo from far of the world and its trade . . .
Murmur of bees in the air; the slow warmth of the
   sunlight;
Ease and forgetting well won ere the long day can fade.

A NATIONAL MARK FOR BRITISH POETRY

The verse herein is warranted
   Of British make and wholesome savour,
On national inspiration fed,
   Entirely free from foreign flavour.

At Runnymede we made King John reluctantly resign
authoritarian powers which went beyond the dotted line;
since then (seven hundred years ago) historians agree
the lovely land of England has been absolutely free.
Our Yankee friends, in this respect, must bear our gentle
    jeers:
they weren't really free for quite five hundred later years;
but on the whole we do not mind if Congress Library
puts Jefferson and John upon a flat equality,
for though the U.S. proved a rather dilatory starter,
Their Declaration sure knocks spots off England's
    famous Charter.

EPSTEIN'S ADAM RUMINATES

God let me—Adam—when he floated Man,
in on the ground floor of the Human Plan;
but shares have slumped; and I, in alabaster,
stare helpless at the proofs of our disaster:
bay-windowed men whose faces shine with food
enjoying an excursion in the nude,
with restless women, titillated, milling
around me, doubtful if I'm worth their shilling.
Old Adam plain I see in the hot gaze
of men still living in primeval days;
Eve, as I knew her, in the sidelong glance
of women eager for the serpent's dance.
I hear their chatter as they pass me by:
the silly-clever and the sensual-sly;

the earnest student babbling from his book;
the parson, black-clothed, cawing like a rook;
and never, in that multi-varied voice,
is one that bids my mournful heart rejoice;
not one that nourishes a hope in me
of that superior race that was to be . . .

O, Jacob Epstein, God, or Whom-you-will,
put once again this people through your mill;
but till they bear some toolmarks of the Master,
let me not live, even in alabaster.

TO THE B.B.C. NIGHTINGALE

Songster, whom poets love to sing,
One bard bewails the woeful thing:
Your notes at secondhand now ring,
    Electrically amplified.

O, gentle bird, what must befall
The intimacy of your call
When lazy millions hear you bawl
    Mechanically far and wide?

We who have hymned your evening joys
See you become a background noise,
A slave to Someone and His Boys:
    You whom we almost deified!

Forgive us, Philomel, that we
Your native woods so seldom see:
We send you, through the B.B.C.,
    Sympathy for your wounded pride.

What, congratulate our sage
On the death-approaching age?
Would the hair still glimmered red
On his laurel-crownéd head!
Would the witches with the shears
Had forgotten half his years!

VESUVIUS ON THE RADIO

Hence, rattled peas and thunder born of tin!
Begone, ye fakers of the disc-and-pin!
Vesuvius speaks, and all our hats we doff
In homage to the chief of Noises-Off.

LINES ON THE OPENING OF A NEW TOWN ON THE SITE OF CIRCE'S LEGENDARY HOME

Does Circe's spirit still look down
    With yearning for the ancient glory,
And faintly in the mushroom town
    Discern the sties that soiled her story?
Sees she familiars in the horde
    Who chatter, where Ulysses sought her,
Of central heat, inclusive board,
    And bedrooms blessed with running water?

LINES ON THE LATE GABRIEL FAHRENHEIT

When Gabriel had calenture
  (An overdose of Sol),
They had to take his temperature
  With tubes of alcohol;

And while the lad with fever burned,
  Now flushing, now grown pale,
His little mind unconscious spurned
  Their thermometric scale.

So Mr. F., grown up, and free
  To put his world in joint,
Swapped alcohol for mercury
  And changed the freezing point.

A CHARM FOR THE COMMON COLD

Gentle pill and healing draught,
Hence this painful feeling waft;
  Take this awful sneeze away:
  Let me have some ease to-day.
May this thrice repeated dose
Cure my cough and dry my nose:
  Menthol, Mistol, Aspirin!
  Be my comfort till I win.

Your aching head's about to split?
    You're sick of quinine tots?
Come, come, my lad: you must admit
    Measles is worse, with spots.

Quick death is all your present hope:
    Deeper each hour your dumps;
But such light blues would have more scope
    If you were down with mumps.

With G.P.I., or twisted gut,
    Jaundice or smallpox, you
Would have real cause for grousing, but
    You've only got the 'flu!

THE SEASIDE PIER

I do not like the seaside pier,
Where concerts all are "rather mere";
Where hateful fellows, with a leer,
Point cameras when I appear;
And where, in alcove lurking near,
An artist (gone to seed, I fear!)
Cuts silhouettes and sells 'em dear;
Where blowsy females, in the sere,
Are telling mugs their past career;
Where grubby children loudly cheer
As towards the slot machines they steer;
Where even ozone smells like beer . . .
Go, call the boss and let him hear:
I hate his silly seaside pier!

A NATIONALIST NATIONAL ANTHEM

O happy land of England,
From foreign evils free!
Who press her sod, we pray thee, God,
That right with British justice shod
Shall tread where we have always trod
To save our land for thee.

O make the men of England
Wise rulers of the earth!
Be theirs, O Lord, the flaming sword
Resolving aliens' rude discord,
To force from foreign laws abhorred
Respect for England's worth.

O bless the soul of England
And keep it pure and true!
Let no foul drain from foreign main
Turn our rich blood to sickly stain:
Preserve in us the English strain
In all we say and do.

KIPLING OVERRATED

Why do I think Kipling overrated
and inadequately hated?
Let me suck up a good red nibful
before I slop a bibful.

Not Peter Pan, but Kipling
was the eternal stripling:
his failure to grow up
has often caused me to throw up.

He believed glory
had to be gory,
like a boy of eighteen
(if you see what I mean).

It might be said
he hadn't an idea in his head
that wasn't mouldier
than a dead Crimean soldier;

but he had the happy knack
of disguising this lack
with a slick spatter
of technical patter.

Nevertheless, even this
was largely hit-or-miss,
and certainly his geography
wasn't nearly as good as his orthography.

God knows
he wrote technically sound prose;
but his narrative nuts have more colonels
than kernels.

And now
allow
me, before anyone says, Stow it!
to attack his reputation as a poet.

Ungrudgingly I admit
he made an occasional hit
with a song
(though it was usually too long);

and one serious hymn
had sense as well as vim
(but they say
he wanted to throw this away!).

He expressed nostalgia
—a little like neuralgia—
for bits of Britain
with which he had been bitten;

but on the whole
he had not the poet's universal soul
and always wanted to sing it
and swing it.

In fact,
and speaking entirely without tact,
his metrical England
was little better than Jingle-land.

Catchwords and zippy rhymes
for *The Times*
are not enough
to sustain for long his poetic bluff.

I shall be happily resigned if what I've said
is taken as red,
since Kipling himself was so nauseatingly true
blue.

GREEDY RICHARD

Richard was not a normal lad:
a sad food-complex Richard had:
instead of playing in the street,
he stayed indoors to eat—and eat!
and, though uncomfortably tight,
he ate while there was food in sight.
The lunch they packed him, as a rule,
was swallowed on the way to school,
and when 'twas time to eat the meal
poor Dick was faint and had to steal!
The neighbours as they watched him feed
said what was wrong with Dick was greed;
but Richard's parents knew that that
was but the surface cause of fat;
and they selected from a list
a foreign psycho-analyst,
who took the strain off Richard's seams
by analysing Richard's dreams,
and promised, with a hopeful smirk,
to guide the lad from food to work . . .
Thus for a fifty-guinea fee
The boy became like you and me;
but O, how his dear mother loathes
the task of taking-in his clothes!

THE FLEA

When children, brought up rich and free,
are bitten by the common flea,
their parents should ascribe the blame

to sheer neglect to Play the Game.
For fleas have one redeeming trend:
it is, to shun the town's West End
and, when untempted, solely bat-
ten on the proletariat.
But there! If John despises nurse
and goes with kids from Bow, or worse,
he can't complain, though highly *natus*,
that vulgar fleas mistake his status
and exercise their legal right
to One Experimental Bite . . .
And John not only feels the pang,
but lets his class down with a bang.

MISS PICKERING

Miss Pickering's angelic wings
were earned by looking into things;
by knocking people up at night
to indicate a thread of light;
by stopping Bernard Shaw to ask
why he dispensed with his gas-mask;
by snooping in the local pub
and pricing other people's grub;
but, scolding once a sand-bag filler,
she met her match: he was a killer!
Behind the barrage at the Bank
Miss Pickering's remains grow rank.

Sipping his pint of old and mild
just like some large, precocious child,
Old Percy set, with wicked glee,
all sorts of rumours floating free:
"They say," was how his tales began,
or maybe "My wife knows a man . . .";
but when he mentioned as a fact
a war-time Prohibition Act,
a carpet salesman, playing darts,
pierced Percy in his vital parts.

Moral

We thought that every schoolboy knew
even a rumour should *sound* true.

MATILDA

Before the age of five, Matilda Mead
from voice repressions was entirely freed;
and, primed with most distressing tricks,
recited "Dauber" at the age of six.
At seven, though gravely warned by brother Percy,
her tonsils throbbed "The Everlasting Mercy".
At eight, still craving adenoidal glory,
she started strong on "Minnie Maylow's Story";
but half-way through (sound here no tragic note)
the Laureate's friends rose up and cut her throat.

DEAR LITTLE AUDREY

Dear little Audrey, with smiling aplomb,
Blew up her aunt with a dear little bomb;
But as she was laughing herself into fits,
She found poor old uncle mixed up with the bits.

*   *   *   *

And so Audrey learnt, that in murder for one,
The bomb's a mistake: she has now bought a gun.

A BALLADE OF THE SEASIDE IN AUGUST

I do not share the highbrow spleen
    For places where the people flock,
Nor do I know just what they mean
    By putting August in the dock.
    I love to see the crowds amok
In August, where there's sea and sand,
    Pierrots and pictures (let them mock!)
And boarding houses and a band.

I do not turn a sickly green
    To see an infant sucking rock:
No penny-in-the-slot machine
    Has ever given me a shock.
    I like to see the beach a-block
With gay girl-bathers, pink or tanned,
    And children asking what's o'clock?
And boarding houses and a band.

Here in the star-lit evening scene
    In friendly shadows lovers lock,
And I the stubble'd radiance glean
    Of ecstasy from hearts a-knock.
    I plunge in August's golden crock,
Find warmth and waves by breezes fanned,
    Bright faces, sterling human stock—
And boarding houses and a band.

Envoy

Dictator, if in power you mean
    To strike at joy with heavy hand,
Let be the August seaside scene,
    And boarding houses and a band.

A BALLADE OF SOLITARY MEALS

Let other men make dinner dates
    With dear old pals or bits of fluff,
And tempt the gastronomic fates
    In restaurants, where meat is tough:
    Go call who will the bourgeois bluff
Of tables which are said to groan
    With wild excess beyond enough:
I much prefer to dine alone.

Not mine the gloom that inspissates,
    Lacking this party-feeling stuff:
My cynic spirit contemplates
    With joy the solitary trough—
    A simple dish or two, *quant suff.*,
Brave thoughts for seasoning—my own.
    Most table-talk is merely guff:
I much prefer to dine alone.

My ivory tower has golden gates:
    When thoughts are grim and times are rough,
I prop a book among the plates,
    Nor heed splashed gravy on my cuff;
    And though they call me surly chuff
Who wish to pick, with me, a bone,
    My course is laid; I will not luff:
I much prefer to dine alone.

Envoy

Prince, if some guest your meal awaits,
    I'd have my private wishes known:
Don't count on me for dinner dates:
    I much prefer to dine alone.

A BALLADE OF BROWN AND JONES AND ROBINSON

Your Cholmondeleys, Montmorencys, Beaulieus,
    Bohuns,
    Are highly ornamental to the view:
They lapped refinement out of silver spoons
    And old tradition says their blood is blue.
    They bear them well, but neither bake nor brew;
And spend their skill avoiding things "not done";
    So when we have a job of work to do
We call on Brown and Jones and Robinson.

Brown can't afford to cultivate Sassoons;
    Jones, careless fellow, drops an aitch or two;
Though Robinson is surety for some boons,
    The clothes he wears are always far from new.
    They ride a Pegasus that never flew—
Manners and morals hopelessly homespun;
    But when we bite off more than we can chew,
We call on Brown and Jones and Robinson.

Our highbrows strike the lyre in strange, wild tunes
  Which seldom wake response in me or you:
Their lyrics, like the old Druidic runes,
  Are cryptograms as clear as melted glue;
  And though we pay them honour more than due,
The confidence we have in them is none.
  For statements that are clear, precise and true,
We call on Brown and Jones and Robinson.

Envoy

Dictator, with a one-class heaven in view,
  We do not envy you your bit of fun
If, taken in by brass and buttons, you
  Dispense with Brown and Jones and Robinson.

IX
TAILPIECE

BANK HOLIDAY ON PARNASSUS

Most kindly the Muses,
  Of Parnassus Mount,
(Where Apollo's mob boozes
  At poetry's fount)
Make room for us trippers
  On Bank Holiday,
With missus and nippers
  And nothing to pay.
There's only one warning
  (And it gets a titter):
Each one by next morning
  Must pick up his litter.
The rule and its fitness
  Let others repine:
You'll all bear me witness,
  I've gathered up mine.